Darjeeling: The Sanitarium of Bengal, and Its Surroundings - Primary Source Edition

R D. O'Brien

Lanman.

Darjeeling, Mar. 1889.

DARJEELING

THE

SANITARIUM OF BENGAL;

AND

ITS SURROUNDINGS,

BY

R. D. O'BRIEN, M.B.

With a Map of the Darjeeling District.

Calcutta:
W. NEWMAN & Co., LD., 4, DALHOUSIE SQUARE.

1883.

DARJEELING

THE

SANITARIUM OF BENGAL;

AND

ITS SURROUNDINGS,

BY

R. D. O'BRIEN, M.B.

With a Map of the Darjeeling District.

Calcutta:
W. NEWMAN & Co., Ld., 4, Dalhousie Square.

1883.

PRINTED BY W. NEWMAN & CO., LD.,
AT THE CAXTON STEAM PRINTING WORKS, 4, DALHOUSIE SQUARE, CALCUTTA.

PREFACE.

MRS. AVERY'S "Up in the Clouds" being out of print, as well as out of date, the writer was asked by Messrs. W. Newman & Co. to prepare for them a more modern Hand-book which would be useful to visitors to what has been truly called the Malvern of Bengal.

If this little book fulfils even a portion of the object with which it is written, the author will be more than satisfied.

DARJEELING,
August, 1883.

CONTENTS.

HAND-BOOK TO DARJEELING.

CHAPTER I.

CALCUTTA TO SILIGURI.

THE voyager to Darjeeling, whether in search of health or pleasure, leaves the Sealdah Terminus of the Northern Bengal Railway by mail train at 3 P.M., and after a tolerably rapid run reaches the right bank of the Ganges at Damookdea in the evening, where he finds a ferry steamer in waiting to carry him up the river to Sara on the left bank, where the southern terminus of the Northern Bengal State Railway is situated. A fairly good dinner is obtainable on board the steamer at a moderate price. From Sara to Siliguri, which is the northern terminus of this railway, the traveller journeys along a metre gauge line, and if the oscillation is rather unpleasant to those accustomed to the broad gauge, the carriages are certainly most comfortable, and it is quite possible to enjoy a sound sleep in them all the way to Jalpaiguri, which is reached generally a little before 6 A.M., and where a very acceptable cup of tea or coffee is obtainable. Siliguri is reached in about one hour, and there is a really excellent refreshment-room at the station, where the traveller will find a very good *chota hazri* waiting for him, and plenty of time to do it justice. At Siliguri the newly completed Himalayan Railway commences, and the traveller is landed at his destination in Darjeeling at 4 P.M.; having travelled the whole distance from Calcutta comfortably and even luxuriously.

This is a very great contrast to travelling to Darjeeling in what is miscalled the "good old days." Before the completion of the Northern Bengal Railway, people wishing to reach Darjeeling were obliged to proceed from Calcutta to Sahibgunge, a distance of 220 miles from the Howrah terminus of the E. I. Railway; thence by ferry steamer to Caragola (a tiresome journey of five hours, and often more) where the unfortunate travellers were disembarked on the river side, and were often obliged to wade a mile or more through the sand under a blazing sun. From thence the route lay along the Ganges-Darjeeling road, *viâ* Purneah, Kissengunge, and Titalaya to Siliguri. This tiresome journey was performed in a jolting ramshackle dâk gharry, and on arriving at Siliguri even the most robust felt as if every bone in his body had been dislocated. From Siliguri there was another 48 miles, ride in a tonga to be accomplished before the jaded wayfarer reached Darjeeling. All this is fortunately changed, and, judging from the crowds of visitors who now visit the sanitarium, the alteration for the better has been thoroughly appreciated by the public of Bengal.

The scenery along the Northern Bengal Railway is just as monotonous as it is in any other portion of Lower Bengal; a huge flat plain stretching on either side as far as the eye can reach, varied here and there by large jheels, where flocks of duck, teal, and, in the season, snipe abound. Here and there, villages surrounded by bamboos, and an occasional mango tope.

A brief description of this railway may be of interest to the reader. The first trial surveys were made in 1870, from Rampore Beauleah to Titalaya, and between Khustia, Rungpore, and Eugwa. Fresh survey operations were undertaken in 1871, and trial lines were run from Sadamara on the Corasagar river to Siliguri, and from Dhapri on the Ganges to Rungpore and Siliguri. Three months after Major (now Lieutenant-Colonel) Lindsay took charge of the surveys, and it was by him that the line was completed. Sir George Campbell, then Lieutenant-Governor of Bengal, suggested the present line, but actual work was not commenced until the outbreak of the Bengal famine in 1874, when construction was begun as a famine relief work. The construction of the line really began during the season 1875-6, and it was completed in 1878, or in less than three working seasons. Owing to the shortness of the season during which work would be carried on—only four months in the year—to the unhealthiness of the low-lying district through which the line passes, the scarcity of labour, and the large amount of bridging to be done—the rapid completion of this line reflected the highest credit on the engineering staff. The line was formally opened by Sir Ashley Eden, then Lieutenant-Governor of Bengal, on the 18th January, 1878.

CHAPTER II.

THE MOUNTAIN RAILWAY.

HAVING breakfasted, the traveller next proceeds to see his light baggage placed on the Darjeeling-Himalayan train, which is in waiting for him at the other side of the platform. This line—two feet gauge—is perhaps one of the greatest feats of engineering skill in the world. It owes its inception to Sir Ashley Eden and to Mr. Prestage, the present Managing Director of the line. Sir Ashley, with his usual practical common sense, recognised the fact that a light railway, if it could only be constructed to Darjeeling, would infinitely develop that town, as well as the country through which it passed, and also put Calcutta and the whole of Lower Bengal in rapid, cheap, and easy communication with its only existing sanitarium. How well-founded his anticipations were has been amply proved by results. Colonel Staunton, R. E., after a careful survey, came to the conclusion that it was quite feasible to run a railway two feet in width along the hill cart road from Siliguri to Darjeeling, and in this opinion most engineers concurred, although many, who knew little or nothing of engineering, scouted the undertaking as impracticable, and prophesied—falsely as results have proved—all sorts of disasters. The Government of Bengal promised to allow the rails to be laid along the road, and guaranteed interest. A Company was formed, the public took up shares in it eagerly, and work was commenced in April, 1879, and the line was finally completed to Darjeeling, a distance of 50 miles, on the 4th July, 1881, when Sir Ashley Eden formally opened it, although trains had been running to the Ghoom station for some months previously. This event was celebrated by a sumptuous tiffin given by the directors to about two hundred guests. In proposing the health of the Lieutenant-Governor, Mr. Prestage, the Managing Director, warmly thanked Sir Ashley Eden for the concession of the line, and pointed out the inmense advantage it would be to the Darjeeling district. In reply Sir Ashley pointed out that the line, with all its difficulties, had only cost £3,000 a mile, and the certainty of a good dividend on the capital being earned, and also drew attention to the immense advantages it would afford to the whole province, both in putting Darjeeling within a twenty-four hours run from Calcutta, as well as in enabling planters in the Darjeeling district to land their produce on the Calcutta market quickly, cheaply, and safely. The capital of the Company was originally 14 lakhs, but has since been increased to 25½ lakhs of rupees, including debentures.

It was originally laid on the hill cart road, but in order to improve the gradient (in some places 1 in 20), and to increase the radii of the numerous curves, many deviations have already been made and are still in course of construction. Practically speaking, the line from the foot of the hills to Gyabari is new. It is expected that when the diversions now being made are completed, a uniform gradient of 1 in 28 from the foot of the hills to Darjeeling will be secured, with the result that the engines will be able to draw heavier loads up the hill. At present (1883) the rolling stock is not equal to the traffic requirements, but this want is being rapidly supplied, and by the end of this year the line will be fully stocked. There were several landslips along the line during last rains, but no accident attended by injury to passengers occurred.

Crossing the Mahanuddi river on a long wooden bridge the railway takes a straight line along the level for about 9 miles to Sookna, where it begins to ascend. From Siliguri to the foot of the hills the line runs through rice fields, with an occasional tea garden on either side, and as the ascent begins a dense sâl forest is passed through. The line now begins to wind in and out along the hill sides, with terrible looking precipices, now on one hand and now on the other. Still steadily ascending the traveller will notice the gradual alteration in the character of the vegetation, the enormous forest trees covered with epiphytes almost to the top, and the mountain streams rushing and roaring down the hill sides and along the bottoms of the deep gorges. The first station reached in the hills is Teendaria, 18 miles from Siliguri, where the train stops for 15 minutes, and where light refreshments are obtainable. The fitting shops of the line are here. A very remarkable piece of engineering is noticeable a little beyond Teendaria, as the line describes a figure of eight. Gyabari, the next station, is reached in about twenty minutes, and here is a reversing station where the train goes back and forwards several times. About two miles from Gyabari, what are locally known as the *goompties* commence. These are long zig-zags along the hill sides for a considerable distance, and a wonderful piece of engineering. From Gyabari, Kursiong is the next station. Here there is a refreshment station. Kursiong from a comparatively small village a few years ago, is now fast growing into a somewhat important hill station. Kursiong is 4,500ft. above the sea level, and from it some splendid views of the plains, as well as of the Balasun valley and Kinchinjunga, are to be had. The traveller, if not pressed for time, will do well to break his journey at this delightful spot. The hotel* is one of the best managed and most comfortable in India. Here there is a very neat little church with a resident clergyman, who is almost entirely supported by the tea planters of this portion of the district. There is also a very excellent school for the education of the children of employés on the State Railways. From Kursiong to Darjeeling the distance is about nineteen miles. The line still runs along the side of the mountain, and the traveller will, on a clear day, obtain most lovely peeps of the valley of the Balasun, as well as of the many tea plantations with their neat white iron-roofed bungalows and factories, which are scattered about all along the valley. The next station reached is Sonadah, 9 miles from Darjeeling; here the train stops about ten minutes. Sonadah is but a small dirty native bazaar, but about two miles below isHope Town, a small settlement of European Tea-planters, with a very neat church. This settlement was

* The Clarendon Hotel, Proprietor, Mr. Roberts. The trains always stop at the Hotel door.

formed some twenty years ago, but for some reason, not easy to account for—it never made much progress, and the tea crash in 1865-66 ruined nearly all the originators of the colony. From Sonadah to Ghoom, the next station, it is usually found that the road is enveloped in dense fog, and that the temperature is almost unpleasantly low even in the middle of summer. The cause is probably the dense forest on the western slopes of Mount Sinchul condensing the moisture in the atmosphere. Passing through the village of Jore Bungalow, a collection of filthy tumble-down huts, the station of Ghoom is reached. This is the highest point on the line, (7,400 feet), and is certainly the highest railway station in the Old World, if not in the universe. This is the most convenient station for passengers for Jellapahar to alight at. From here the line descends rapidly towards Darjeeling, 4 miles off. At this point the Balasun valley is left, and the line passes along the valley of the Little Runjeet. An occasional glimpse of the barracks of Jellapahar, perched high on the top of the mountain on the right hand side, will now be obtained, and on the left-hand side will be seen numerous tea gardens in the foreground, with Mount Tongloo and the great Singalila range for a background. About a mile and-a-half from Ghoom the first view of Darjeeling is obtained; and it certainly is a most striking one. The hillside is dotted over with picturesque villa residences, and if the weather is at all clear, the mighty snow peaks are clearly visible.

Arrived at Darjeeling the traveller, as soon as he alights from the train, is almost mobbed by a crowd of importunate, dirty coolies, all anxious to take charge of him and his baggage, and to demand exorbitant prices for doing so. Here it may be as well to advise intending visitors to Darjeeling to make sure of accommodation beforehand, as it has often happened that people have found themselves landed in the town, and have had the greatest difficulty in getting even a "shake down," in the literal acceptation of the word. This warning should be particularly borne in mind during the Dusserah holidays.

Darjeeling 7,200 ft. Murray's
Bengal p. 146.

CHAPTER III.

THE DISTRICT OF DARJEELING.

THE Darjeeling District is situated to the north of zillahs Purneah and Rungpore, and is the north-western district of the Rajshahye and Cooch Behar Division. It lies between 26° 30' 50" and 27°13' 5" north latitude, and between 88° 2' 45" and 88° 56' 35" east longitude. It contains a total area, according to a return by the Surveyor-General of India in January, 1876, of 1,234 square miles; and according to the last Census a total population of 157,038 souls; and is divided into two portions—the northern, consisting of a succession of hill and valley with an average of from 4,000 to 9,000 feet above the sea level, and the southern (or Morung), of the skirts of the first range of the Himalaya, and the plains lying between that and Zillah Rungpore. On the north, the rivers Rumam, Great Runjeet, and Teesta, divide this district from Sikkim on the east, the rivers De-chee and Ne-chee separate it from Bhootan, on the west the river Mechi, and a lofty chain of hills divide it from Nepal. From the source of the Mechi northward, the ridge of the Tongloo and Phulloot mountains carries the western boundary north to the river Rumam; to the south the district is contiguous with the Zillahs Rungpore and Purneah. In the report of the Superintendent, Dr. Campbell, of the 23rd May, 1851, it is stated that the southern tract, called the Morung, formerly belonged to Sikkim, it was ceded to the British Government by treaty with Nepal in 1816, and at the same time granted to the Sikkim Rajah. Its total area is 4,000 square miles. The upper portion of the Morung, lying immediately at the base of the mountains, is covered with forest and jungle, but much of it is suited for the growth of cotton, as well as of tea. It has a very fertile soil, and is inhabited by two tribes, the Mechis and the Dhimals. These tribes do not suffer from the unhealthy character of the Terai, but get ill at once on leaving it for the open plains, or the mountains. They are much diminished now, having become absorbed in a great measure with the other coolies employed in the tea industry, many also having left the district to settle in Jalpaiguri and other places. The original history of the occupation of the tract of land called British Sikkim is this :—At the close of the war with Nepal in 1817, it was ceded by that government to the British, the original object being to hedge in Nepal by an ally, and prevent her extending her boundary towards the East. The following is a copy of the Treaty executed at Titalya in February, 1817.

"Treaty, covenant, or agreement, entered on by Capt. Barre Latter, agent on the part of H. E. the Right Honorable the Earl of Moira, K. G., Governor-General, &c., &c., and by Nazir Chama Jiragen, and Macha Jimbah, and Llama Duchim Longdoo, Deputies on the part of the Rajah of Sikkimputtee, being severally authorised and duly appointed for the above purposes.

Art. 1st.—The Honorable East India Company cedes, transfers, and makes over in full sovereignty to the Sikkimputtee Rajah, his heirs or successors, all the hilly or mountainous country situated to the eastward of the Mechi river, and to the westward of the Teesta river, formerly possessed and occupied by the Rajah of Nepal, ceded to the Honorable East India Company by the treaty of peace signed at Segouli.

Art. 2.—The Sikkimputtee Rajah engages for himself and his successors to abstain from any acts of aggression or hostility against the Goorkhas or any other State.

Art. 3.—That he will refer to the arbitration of the British Government any disputes or questions that may arise between his subjects and those of Nepal, or any other neighbouring state, and abide by the decision of the British Government.

Art. 4.—He engages for himself and successors, to join the British troops with the whole of his military force when employed within the hills, and in general to afford the British troops every aid and facility in his power.

Art. 5.—That he will not permit any British subject, nor the subject of any European or American State, to reside within his dominions without the permission of the English Government.

Art. 6.—That he will immediately seize and deliver up any dacoits, or notorious offenders, that may take refuge within his territories.

Art. 7.—That he will not afford protection to any defaulters of revenue or other delinquents, when demanded by the British Government through their accredited agents.

Art. 8.—That he afford protection to merchants and traders from the Company's provinces; and he engages that no duties shall be levied on the transit of merchandize beyond the established custom at the several golahs or marts.

Art. 9.—The Honorable East India Company guarantees to the Sikkimputtee Rajah, and his successors, the full and peaceable possession of the tract of hilly country specified in the first article of the present agreement.

Art. 10.—This treaty shall be ratified and exchanged by the Sikkimputtee Rajah within one month from the present date, and the counterpart, when confirmed by H. E. the Right Honorable the Governor-General, shall be transmitted to the Rajah.

Done at Titalya this 10th day of February, 1817, answering to the 9th of Phagon, 1873 Sumbut, and to the 30th of Maugh, 1293, Bengal era."

About the month of February, 1828, Mr. J. W. Grant, c. s., then resident at Malda, and Capt. Lloyd, employed in settling the boundary between Nepal and Sikkim, made an excursion as far as Choutong (a few miles west of Darjeeling), and were struck with the idea of what a suitable place the latter would be for a sanitarium. These gentlemen brought the matter to the notice of the Governor-General, Lord William Bentinck. Major Herbert, Deputy Surveyor-General, was then directed to survey the Sikkim Hills, which he did with a party in 1830; he concluded his survey during the season, and submitted his reports to Government.

These reports were forwarded to the Directors of the East India Company, who directed that the Indian Government should found, if possible, a sanitarium at Darjeeling for the benefit of the troops, and also as a permanent Cantonment. Some time was lost in the necessary arrangements, but in 1835, the tract of land including Darjeeling and the Western and North-Western slopes from Sinchul, and the approaches to the plains, was ceded by treaty with the Rajah of Sikkim, the British Government granting him a compensation of Rs. 3,000 a year. The following is the deed of grant, which conveyed this valuable tract of land into the hands of the British for a mere nominal compensation. "The Governor-General having expressed a desire for the possession of the hill of Darjeeling, on account of its cool climate, for the purpose of enabling the servants of his Government suffering from sickness to avail themselves of its advantages.

"I, the Sikkimputtee Rajah, out of friendship to the said Governor-General, hereby present Darjeeling to the East India Company, that is, all the land south of the Great Runjit river, east of the Balasun, Kahail, and Little Runjit rivers, and west of the Rungno and Mahanuddi rivers.

"Seal of the Rajah affixed to the document.

"Dated 99th Maugh, Sumbut 1891 (answering to our A. D., 1835)."

The station was inaugurated by Captain Lloyd (in charge of N.-E. frontier) and Dr. Chapman, going up to Darjeeling and living there, exploring, building, clearing, &c. In 1839 Captain Lloyd made over the station to Dr. A. Campbell, who having been resident at Nepal for some time, was transferred to Darjeeling as its first Superintendent. To him is due the fact of the prosperity of the settlement; he was Superintendent for twenty-two years, and during that time made roads, bridged torrents, organized the bazaar, built houses, the Cutcherry and Church, a convalescent depôt at Jellapahar for soldiers, introduced English flowers and fruits, experimented on tea seed being grown, encouraged commerce, and created a revenue. When Dr. Campbell took charge there were not more than twenty families in the whole tract of hills. The Morung portion of the district, as also the Rs. 3,000 a year, was taken from the Rajah of Sikkim, in consequence of his having seized and detained in confinement two British subjects, *viz.*, Dr. Campbell, the Superintendent of the district, and Dr. Hooker, the well-known naturalist, on a botanical and geological tour, without any tenable reason, and while travelling peaceably through the country.*

The following account will give a general idea of the soil, productions, &c., of this interesting place:—

"The soil is stiff red or yellow clay, with gneiss rock lying under it, and in some places coming to the surface. Gneiss crumbled in the form of sand is met with in different parts of the hills. Where the jungle has not been cleared, there is a fine surface soil of vegetable mould, ranging from six to twelve inches in depth. This yields one or two fair crops; where, however, the vegetable soil is washed away by the rains, little is left but the primitive clay, with here and there the bald rock standing out. The only minerals at present found in the hills are copper, iron, coal, and manganese; they have not, however, as yet, been found in sufficient quantities to remunerate the miner. Lime is found in the valleys.

"The Sikkim territory abounds with the following timber,

* In Dr. Hooker's Himalayan Journal, a long accurate account of the above is given.

fruit and flowering trees and plants. From 12,000 to 10,000 feet above the sea are found fir trees *(Abies Webbiana)*, Dwarf Rhododendron, Aromatic Rhododendron, several other sorts of Rhododendrons, Juniper, Holly, Arboreous Rhododendron, Red Currant bushes, Cherry trees, Pear, Daphne or Paper tree, Potentilla, Creeping Raspberry, Hypericum, Ranunculus, Geranium, Veronica, Polyanthus, one buff-colored and two lilac Primroses, Violets, Dack, *Aconitum pulmatum* or Bikh plant, and *Aconitum Ferox*, (from the root of which a deadly poison is extracted), dwarf Cheem Bamboo, Iris Anemone, (blue and white) Arisanna, Balsum, Heartsease, two kinds of grass, Carex, Moss and Lichens.

"From 10,000 to 9,000 feet, Oak, Chestnut, Magnolia, Arboreous Rhododendron, Michelia or Chumpa, Olive, Fig *(Ficus goolooreea)*, Laurel (Cinnamonum and Cassia), Barberry, Maple, Nettles, Lily of the Valley, Cheem Bamboo, Rue, Rhubarb, *Androumela Celastrus*, White Rose.

"From 9,000 to 8,000 feet, Maple, Rhododendron, Michelia, Oak, Laurels, Lime trees, Dogwood, Veberneum, Hydrangea, Helwingia, Ginseng, Symplocus, Celastrus, Vaccinium Serpeus.

"From 8,000 to 6,500 feet, Elder, Peach, Oak, Chestnut, Maple, Alder, Michelia, Olive, Walnut, Toon, Hydrangea, Birch, Holly, Erythrina, Magnolia, all the English flowers, Rue, Raspberry, three kinds, Strawberry, Rhubarb, Potato, Hypericum, Polygona of many kinds and which form the principal underwood at Darjeeling, Wild Ginger, Osbechia, Brambles, Thunbergia, Wormwood *(Artemesia Santonine)*.

"From 6,500 to 4,000 feet—6,500 feet is the upper limit of Palms, Alder, Oak, Maple, Birch, Acacia, Dalbergia, Terminalia, Tree fern, Plantain, Wild Vine, Bignonia, Holly, Elder, Barbadoes Cherry tree, Olive, Hydrangea, Pear trees, Pepper, Pothos covering whole trees, Menisperma, Helwingia, Pendulous mosses, Lichens, Arums of many kinds, Arisooema, Calami or Rattan, Caryota Palm, Aquilaria, Myrsine, Enbelia, Ardisia, Sonneratia. 5,000 feet is about the upper limit of cultivation for Rice, Barley, two species of Buckwheat, Murwa, Indian-corn, Junera, Yam, Brinjal, Bhang, Fennel, Cummin, Mint, and Rue.

"From 4,000 to 1,000 feet Gordonia, Pandanus, Sâl, Toon, Bombax or cotton tree, Banian and other Figs, Orange, Peach, Pine *(Pinus Longifolia)*, Banana, Lemon, Wormwood 12 feet in height.

"From 1,000 to the plains, Figs of five kinds, Date trees *(Phœnix)*, Wallichia Caryotoides, Cycas pectinata, twelve kinds of Bamboo, Phylanthus Emblica, Grislea, Marlea, Sterculia, Trophis Sissen, Butea, Mimosa Catechu, Soap worts, Terebenthaceæ, Symplocus, climbing Leguminosa, Cucurbitacea, Wild Mulberry, three kinds of nettle, Boehmeria Euphorbia, Turmeric, Ginger, many kinds of grass in the Morung, some 20 feet in height, Terrestrial orchids, Ferns, Bondellata, Randia, Oak.

Nearly all the above are marked according to Dr. Hooker. There are several species of Oak. Five are known as yielding good timber. The Oak of the Himalaya cannot, however, compete with the sturdy British oak. The damp appears to deprive it of the strength and durability for which its English namesake is famous. Chestnut is an excellent wood, used for building purposes. The nut is small and sweet. Birch, two species. Maple, two species. Sâl, which is one of the best Indian woods, grows abundantly in the neighbourhood of Punkabari. It is also found on the other side of Darjeeling, near the Runjeet. Toon grows to a large size in the lower districts. The Wild Mango grows between Kursiong and Punkabari. The fruit is small, cylindrical in form, and has not much of the flavor of the mango of the plains. Rhododendron, white and red. Darjeeling appears to be about the lowest elevation at which these shrubs grow luxuriantly. There is quite a forest of them on Fongloo. It grows to a gigantic size, and flowers in April and May. The wood is white, light, and durable. Walnut, a very handsome wood, used for furniture and house building. Champ, a yellow cross-grained wood, excellent for ceiling, flooring, chimney-pieces, doors, and windows. Magnolia, a large handsome tree, white-flowered and highly scented, flowers in the spring, scenting the air with its fragrance. The popularly called Lotus tree, a large handsome tree, flowers in the spring, it bears a profusion of large, lotus-like pink flowers. When in full bloom, this tree is really the queen of the forest; it belongs to the genus Magnolia. Sycamore, somewhat like the Plane tree. The wood is good. The natives use the leaves as a substitute for tea. Holly, a large, handsome plant, and especially so in the winter, when it is in full leaf, and its branches covered with scarlet berries. There is a species of Olive; the fruit is as large as a plum. The wood, though not durable, is used for door-posts and out-buildings. Semul, well known in the plains for its cotton, grows at an elevation of 3,500 feet. Figs, two species, edible, ripen in August. The Pimento tree bears a spicy berry, which has somewhat the flavor of strong orange peel; it is used medicinally by the natives. The Paper tree, three species: the yellow, white, and scarlet flowered. The yellow flowered thrives at an elevation of about 5,000 feet. The paper made from this tree is coarse and dark coloured. The whitish and pink is abundant; this thrives in a belt embracing 2,000 feet in elevation, that of Darjeeling, 7,257 feet, being the centre; it is the most abundant of the species. The scarlet flowered is found on higher elevations such as Sinchul. Olea Fragrans is abundant about Darjeeling, it is sweet-scented, and flowers in October. Pines are found near the Runjeet. Wild Cherry is abundant below Darjeeling. The Barberry is indigenous to the district, the fruit is equal to British fruit, the wood is green, and used for dyeing purposes. There is also a yellow, durable wood, very offensive when fresh cut, called by some "Stink Wood."

The Tea plant is not indigenous to the Darjeeling district. It was introduced by Dr. Campbell. But this shrub deserves a chapter to itself.

Darjeeling Hill Station and Sanitarium.

Rainfall in Inches.				Average Temperature in Shade.						Prevailing Winds.		
January to May.	June to September.	October to December.	Total.	May.		July.		December.		January to May.	June to September.	October to December.
				Minimum.	Maximum.	Minimum.	Maximum.	Minimum.	Maximum.			
14·70	100·09	0·38	115·17	51·9	65·9	59·4	70·5	96·9	52·4	S. W. W. & E.	E. & S. E.	E. S. W. & W.

Mean 56° Fahrenheit.

CHAPTER IV.

THE STATION OF DARJEELING.

THE town, if it can really be called one, consists of a bazaar occupying the centre of a basin, around which, on the hill sides, are scattered the residences of the European inhabitants, and the villas occupied by visitors to the sanitarium during the "season," which begins in April and ends in October. The mean temperature of the station is 56° Fahr., and the average rainfall 120 inches. Rain or snow generally falls in Darjeeling in December or January, and hail storms with high wind are common in March or April.

POPULATION.

According to the Census of 1881, which is generally acknowledged to be very fairly correct, the population of the district was as follows :—

Darjeeling Thannah.

Males	38,422
Females	29,826
Total ...	68,248

Kursiong Thannah.

Males	9,812
Females	6,399
Total ...	16,211

Phasidena Thannah.

Males	... ...	41,276
Females	... ...	31,363
	Total ...	72,639

Total population of the district, 157,098.

The Census of 1872 gave a total population of 94,712 souls, so that the increase during nine years was 62,326. This extraordinary increase was entirely due to the large amount of land cleared for tea cultivation in 1873-4-5.

The languages spoken are Bengali, Bhootea, Hindi, Lepcha, and Nepalese.

The Aboriginal Tribes inhabiting the District are the Lepcha, Aka, Dhimal, Mechi, Murmi, and Urava. Nepalese, Bhooteas, and Thibetans form the great majority of the foreign element.

CLIMATE.

The climate of Darjeeling is essentially a moist one, and during February, June, July, August, and September, clouds are generally prevalent. There are practically three seasons—spring, the rainy season, and winter. Spring may be said to begin about the third week of February, and lasts until the end of May, and the rainy season from June to the end of October. The following are the maximum and minimum temperatures of the different months:—

	Maximum.	*Minimum.*		*Maximum.*	*Minimum.*
January	62°	30°	July	75°	56°
February	63°	32·2°	August	73°	57°
March	72°	32·2°	September	76°	52°
April	69°	43·4°	October	73°	44°
May	73°	43·4°	November	64°	39°
June	78°	55°	December	58°	33°

During the spring months the mornings and evenings are cool, but during the day time the sun comes out in full force, and the heat is often trying. Thunderstorms are frequent during this portion of the year. The rainy season usually sets in early in June, and lasts until the middle of October, and during this period about 100 inches of rain fall, the greatest amount generally falling in July. A great deal has been said and written about the terrible rainfall of Darjeeling during the rainy season, but the accounts are all more or less over-drawn. It is true that the rain comes down in torrents for hours, and sometimes for days together, but it is only in exceptional seasons that it is impossible to get out of the house for a few hours in the twenty-four without fear of getting wet. Somehow, the rain seems to harm nobody if, on returning home after a drenching, the ordinary precaution of changing clothes is adopted.

Winter begins about the end of October, and lasts to about the middle of February. During November and most of December the days are bright and sunny, and the nights clear and frosty. Towards Christmas, rain or snow generally falls, and the weather is usually overcast for a few days, and snow accompanied by a thick, chilling, cutting fog, falls usually towards the end of January or early in February. At this time the climate is most trying, and coughs and colds are prevalent. After the snow has fallen the weather clears up again, and the temperature is most enjoyable.

Medical Aspects.

On account of its elevation Darjeeling is above the reach of malaria, and its equable, though moist climate renders it an excellent sanitarium for Europeans. The mountain breezes are life-giving and charged with ozone, and at almost every inspiration the visitor, whose health has suffered from a long residence on the plains of Bengal, feels as if he were adding days to his life. But the visitor, more or less broken down in constitution, must be cautious if he wants the change of climate to do him good. He must always be warmly clad, never neglect to wear flannel under-clothing, and must eschew cold "tubs." Tubbing in Darjeeling is just as essential to health as it is in any other part of the world, but on no account should a small dash of hot water be forgotten to be added to the cold. The neglect of this precaution is a very frequent cause of liver congestion—for which the climate is generally unfairly blamed. Another precaution to be taken is, not to go out in the middle of the day when the sun is at its height, and when it is quite as trying as in the plains, without some suitable covering for the head. The " Terai hat" is sufficient protection, and so is the " Dr. Tuson's" felt helmet, but without an umbrella a severe headache is frequently the result of venturing out in the sun in a small black hat.

The water-supply of Darjeeling can now compare favorably with that of any Indian station, and with many English towns. The water is brought in pipes from the western face of Mount Sinchul, a distance of some four or five miles, to a large reservoir near " Rockville" just above the Mall, from whence it is distributed throughout the station. The quantity of water available for all purposes is quite equal to the requirements of a population double that of Darjeeling proper, while the quality is irreproachable. Unfortunately, none of the inhabitants have yet seen their way to laying on a water-supply from the mains to their houses. The surplus water is used in flushing the drains, and as they are all open, there can be "no deception" in this matter.

So long ago as 1850 Sir Joseph Hooker described Darjeeling as the paradise of children, and his description of the place holds good to the present day. The children born and reared in Darjeeling are quite as chubby, bright, active, and happy as could be seen in the most favored spots in Europe, while children brought up from the plains of Bengal suffering from anæmia, flabby, pale, fretful, and disinclined to do anything but moan, and worry all who have anything to do with them, soon become models of health and cheerfulness, and run their parents' butcher's bill up in an astonishing way. Considering the large infantile population, the mortality amongst children is almost nominal, as, unlike towns at home, scarlatina is absolutely unknown, and so are most infantile maladies that one has to be prepared for in the old country. Measles and chicken-pox do break out occasionally, but the types of both diseases are wonderfully mild compared with home; and no case is on record of a European, whether child or adult, ever having been attacked with cholera in Darjeeling. The climate was formerly supposed not to have been suited for persons affected with asthma or any organic disease of the lungs, heart, or liver. This has been proved to be a mistake. So-called hill diarrhœa is not nearly so common or so troublesome as at other hill stations. Enlargement of the spleen is always much improved by a stay at Darjeeling, as are all other diseases traceable to malarial poisoning.

ACCOMMODATION.

Although the number of houses in the station has more than doubled within the last three years, persons wishing to rent a house should apply not later than the middle of December. The new semi-detached villas built recently on the Maharajah of Kuch Bihar's property are decidedly the best and neatest in the station. As they are completely furnished, the tenant need bring nothing but his clothes with him. The rents are moderate for Darjeeling. Mr. G. Clark, C.E., who is the model of courtesy, is the agent. At the other end of the station is another collection of houses built by the late David Wilson, of the Great Eastern Hotel. These houses, though old, are maintained in capital repair, are comfortably furnished and well situated. Mr. T. Balmer is the agent. With regard to boarding houses, Darjeeling is fairly well off. "Rockville," charmingly situated on the ridge of the hill, commands a glorious view on all sides. Ladies with delicate children are confidently recommended to go to "Rockville," as Mrs. Houghton, the proprietress, makes children a speciality. It is excellently conducted in every respect; a capital table is kept, the attendance is good, and the charges are moderate. Almost in the centre of the station are the numerous boarding houses owned and managed by the Messrs. Doyle, the well-known *entrepreneurs*. These gentlemen have earned a well-deserved reputation throughout India for the excellent manner in which their boarding houses are conducted; and they can be strongly recommended. "Castleton House," managed by Mrs. Cowham, is a new establishment. The house is well situated, and well managed; can be recommended.

There is only one hotel in Darjeeling at present, but there is every probability of another being built on the *site* at present occupied by the Bengal Secretariat offices, when the latter are removed to "Beechwood." "Woodlands" is capitally managed, and is very comfortable, and has the advantage of being within five minutes walk of the railway station.

In addition to the above there are several houses where visitors are received *en famille*, and made very comfortable.

SERVANTS.

Darjeeling has always been an expensive station, and the completion of the railway seems to have made no appreciable difference in the cost of living. Servants are expensive, and most difficult to manage. A good reliable sirdar bearer should always be brought up from the plains; no others need be, as all the rest are obtainable on the spot. The following is an approximate table of the rate of wages prevailing. It is only possible to give approximate figures, as the rates demanded and paid vary considerably.

Bearer	From	Rs	10 to 12
Khitmutgar	"	"	12 — 14
Cook	"	"	16 upwards
Ayah	"	"	10 to 14
Dhai (with food) ...	"	"	30 — 50
Syce	"	"	8
Leaf Cutter	"	"	7
Dhobi (according to household)	"	"	10 upwards
Bhisti (who serves several houses)		Rs	6 to 10
Mehter		"	12 — 14
Dandy-bearers		"	8 — 10 each
Tailor		"	10 — 18

Many of the hill men make excellent servants. The Bhooteas and Lepchas, when caught young, make excellent cooks and khitmutgars, and they have the advantage of having no caste prejudices, and of being able to turn their hands to any kind of work. The Nepalese make very good bearers and khitmutgars. Bhootea and Lepcha women are capital childrens' ayahs; and if not spoiled by previous mistresses, have no hesitation in undertaking methrani work. Bhooteas will not take syce's work, nor will Lepchas as a general rule, but the Nepalese will do so, and look after the ponies in their charge very well. It is wonderful how they manage to climb up the hills, and what long distances they can travel without fatigue. It is necessary to keep a leaf-cutter for each pony, as there is no green fodder obtainable in Darjeeling, and consequently these men have to go long distances to obtain bamboo leaves, the universal food of ponies in the station. The *puttawallah* is supposed to help the syce in cleaning out the stable in the morning, and to assist in grooming and keeping the horse-gear clean. Bhistis are almost invariably men from the plains, as are the dhobis. The dandy-bearers are either Bhooteas or Lepchas. They are a dirty, impudent, extortionate set as a general rule, but it is hoped that Mr. Macaulay's bill for regulating wages of hill coolies, will have the much-needed effect of clipping their wings. *Ticca* dandy-bearers are almost always available; like the others they are extortionate and impudent. As a rule ladies ought never to venture out of the station without the escort of a gentleman when carried by *ticca* dandy-bearers, as these men have a playful habit of putting the dandy down on the road, demanding extra pay, and if their modest request is not complied with, their fair burden, if not escorted by a gentleman, is left to shift for herself on an out-of-the-way road; perhaps in a downpour of rain.

Local Food Supplies.

Animal food of a fair quality is obtainable on paying a good price. The sheep are brought in from Thibet, Nepal, and Sikkim. The Thibet sheep is small, and the mutton of excellent flavor, but unfortunately these sheep will not live in Darjeeling during the rains. The Nepalese sheep is a big Roman-nosed brute, with coarse, flavorless flesh. Good beef is generally obtainable. Pork is obtainable, but the purchaser ought to know from whence it comes, as the hill pig is just as dirty a feeder as his relative of the plains. Hams and bacon of really good quality are obtainable. Poultry is usually brought from Nepal and from the plains. It is impossible to buy a good fat roasting fowl in the bazaar, but most people fatten their own poultry. The same may be said of geese and ducks. The Sikkim cock is a fine bird, and appears, somehow, to have a bit of the Chittagong breed in him. His crow is most extraordinary. He begins like any other chanticleer, but winds up with something between a grunt and a groan. Eggs are plentiful, and as a rule good, but the price runs up terribly sometimes. The milk is always good when the services of the *cow with the iron tail* have not been called in. The Bhootea *gwallahs* are past masters in adulteration. Butter is one of the features of Darjeeling, and if, as is the general rule, it is made on the premises by the household servants, is quite as good as the best English butter. Fish brought up from the Runjeet and Teesta, is often obtainable perfectly fresh and of excellent flavor. Fish is also brought up in ice from Calcutta, and reaches Darjeeling in excellent condition. Vegetables are difficult to obtain as a rule, but all the English vegetables thrive in and around Darjeeling, and are of excellent quality. The Darjeeling potato has been much improved by the importation of English seed. Really excellent potatoes are to be had all the year round. The Bhootea turnip is really delicious, and is in season in November. Oranges are imported in large quantities from Sikkim, and are simply delicious in December and January, but unfortunately for visitors none are obtainable during the rains. The bread supply of Darjeeling is not what it should be, considering the large population of the place. Bread is made at the recently established jail bakery, but the quality of the "staff of life" supplied leaves much room for improvement. Fruit such as plantains, pine apples, pears, peaches (the two latter only fit for stewing), guavas and a yellow raspberry are obtainable, and if the visitor has any friends amongst the tea-planters, he will often be able to taste strawberries. Altogether the present food supply of Darjeeling, in spite of improved means of communication, is not what it might be and ought to be; but there is every reason for hoping that this very serious defect will soon be remedied, as Dr. Greenhill, so well known in Calcutta, has established a farm under European supervision at Nagri, about 10 miles from Darjeeling, from whence all the needs of the station in this respect will be amply supplied.

CHAPTER V.

PUBLIC BUILDINGS AND ESTAPLISHMENTS.

WE take the *Church* (St. Andrew's) first, as it will soon be one of the most conspicuous objects in Darjeeling. It is situated on a knoll under the Observatory Hill and close to the Town Hall. It is a plain, substantial, barn-like building, with a corrugated iron roof. The foundation was laid on St. Andrew's Day, 1843, and the original Church (for this present one is the second on the same site) was built under the superintendence of Captain Bishop, and had to be pulled down some twelve years ago. The more modern structure is almost as plain inside as out, although there is a tolerably good east window, and a few neat tablets on the walls put in to commemorate the virtues of departed Darjeeling worthies. This Church has sittings for about 400 people, but it is becoming more evident daily that, with the rapid increase of population during the last few years, largely increased sitting accommodation must be provided ere long. There is an excellent choir on either side of the Communion Table, and an Organ presented to the Church by Mr.

William Lloyd, who has always been so consistent and so liberal a benefactor to Darjeeling. This Organ has unfortunately never given satisfaction, and has recently been condemned. At present a Campanille is in course of erection on the south side of the Church, which when completed will be about 85 feet high, and will have a peal of bells and a clock.

Next to the Church is the *Town Hall*, socially one of the most important public buildings in Darjeeling. The building is a plain but commodious one, and capitally suited to the purposes for which it is used. This was originally the Cutcherry and Treasury, but has been altered almost out of recognition by those who knew it some years ago. The Town Hall is leased from the Municipality by the Entertainment Committee (of which Mr. G. R. Clarke, C.E., is the popular and energetic Honorary Secretary). This building contains a *bijou* Theatre, where amateur performances are frequently given during the season, as well as afternoon and evening concerts. There is also a noble Ball Room, with one of the best dancing floors out of the presidency towns. There are also reading and other rooms,—the former being well supplied with nearly all the newspapers and periodical literature of the day. Outside the Town Hall are a number of well laid out Lawn Tennis Courts, where this pleasant game is played vigorously every fine day. To become a member of the Entertainment Club one has to be introduced by a member. The subscription is six rupees a month during the "season," with a substantial reduction during the cold weather.

A little beyond the Town Hall towards the N.-W. is *The Shrubbery*, the residence of the Lieutenant-Governor of Bengal during his periodical visits to Darjeeling. This fine and commodious mansion is situated in extensive and prettily laid out grounds. It is two-storied, and occupies the site of a bungalow originally built by Sir Thomas Turton.

The *Eden Sanitarium* (opened to the public towards the end of 1882) occupies an isolated knoll in almost the centre of Darjeeling proper. It has been constructed from designs by Mr. Martin, C.E., the Government Architect. From its position alone, this building would form a striking feature in the Darjeeling landscape; but in addition to this, the erection is of a very handsome and ornate character externally, whilst internally it is admirably suited to the purpose for which it was designed. The history of this Institution, which will, when its advantages are better and more widely known, prove of such incalculable advantage, alike to rich and poor of this province, may be here very briefly touched on. Originally there was no hospital accommodation for Europeans in Darjeeling. The poor had to trust to luck more or less, while the only refuges available for the well-to-do were private dwellings or boarding houses,—the former expensive and uncomfortable at the best, while in the case of the latter the owner, for his own protection, would naturally refuse boarders suffering from either infectious or contagious disease. Seeing this serious want in a Sanitarium, Dr. Purves, the then Civil Surgeon, managed to set apart a couple of rooms in the native hospital for the use of European patients. From this very humble beginning originated the Eden Sanitarium. Dr. Birch, the successor of Dr. Purves, succeeded in equipping a detached building in the native hospital compound for the use of European patients, who were charged a sum *per diem* just sufficient to cover the cost of their maintenance. The wards were always full, and it was then seen that there was an opening for a really large General Hospital in Darjeeling. Sir Ashley Eden, with his characteristic energy, took the scheme up warmly. Government aid was given liberally, the Maharajah of Burdwan headed the list of donations with the munificent sum of Rs. 10,000, and subscriptions flowed in liberally.

The Sanitarium is a two-storied building facing nearly north and south. The front is towards the south, and contains the apartments for the first and second class patients, with sitting and dining rooms, &c., while the wings, running backwards to the north, contain of the wards for the third class patients, sitting and dining rooms, &c. The rooms and wards are all well warmed, ventilated and lighted, and are replete with all modern comforts and conveniences. The Sanitarium is under the superintendence of the Civil Surgeon of Darjeeling, (at present Dr. Joubert) who is assisted by an influential working Committee, and the general internal arrangements are in the hands of a House Surgeon, a Steward, and some trained Sisters from the Lady Canning Home. There is accommodation for 64 patients, of whom 8 (4 male and 4 female) are 1st, 16 (8 male and 8 female) are 2nd, 40 (20 male and 20 female) are 3rd class. The first class patients have each a bed, dressing, and bath room to themselves, with use of the common sitting and dining rooms. The rate for first class patients is eight rupees a day. Two second class patients share a bed-room, with dressing and bath-rooms attached, and use of dining and sitting rooms. The charge for second class patients is four rupees a day. The third class patients occupy four wards in the wings with ten beds in each ward. They have the use of common dining and sitting rooms. The charge for this class is one rupee a day. There is no possible doubt but that in time, and when its many invaluable advantages have become more generally known throughout Bengal, this institution will become a popular resort for all classes of invalids from the plains.

The *Cutcherry* is a long plain building in the bazaar. It was originally built for the accommodations of native travellers, then used as a butcher's shop, after that for some years it was a Town Hall, and destiny has latterly converted it into a cutcherry and treasury. The building is utterly unsuited to the purposes for which it has been adapted, and it is hoped that before long a more suitable building will be erected somewhere else.

The *Post* and *Telegraph Offices* are in one plain building, and are situated immediately below the club.

The *Club* is a very fine and commodious one, and having been specially built for the purpose, it is admirably suited to the requirements of the members. Gentlemen visiting Darjeeling during the season are admitted as temporary members on being properly introduced.

The *Jail*, situated below the Victoria Road, consists of several barracks surrounded by a high red brick wall. The building calls for little or no notice. There is a large bakery in the jail, from whence a large proportion of the bread required for the station, is supplied.

Close to the jail is the *Lloyd Botanic Garden.* This is a piece of ground immediately under the Eden Sanitarium, which was presented to Government by the well known gentleman, whose name it bears. The grounds are well timbered, and are laid out in the most artistic style of landscape gardening, and the flower-beds are constantly blazing with the most attractive varieties of the floral world. In the centre of the garden is a magnificent conservatory, constructed of plate glass and iron, with a very fine transept. This garden is worth while seeing at all times, and is a most pleasant lounge on a fine spring, summer or autumn evening. The Curator is Mr. A. T. Jafferey, who is always pleased to show visitors round the garden. Visitors should not fail to inspect the beautiful collections of dried ferns made by Mrs. Jafferey.

The *Union Chapel* is situated on the Auckland road. It is a plain iron-roofed building, and is available for the worship of Christians of all denominations.

The *Barracks* are situated at *Jellapahar*, above, and about two miles south of Darjeeling proper. Here is accommodation for about 250 men, with a number of women and children. The buildings are plain, small, scattered bungalows, with rubble stone walls and iron-roofs.

The *Railway Station* is a long barnlike construction of wood and iron, situated a few hundred yards to the south of the Darjeeling bazaar.

The *Bazaar* is quite down in the hollow, a square piece of ground flanked on either side by the native shops, and a Hindoo Temple, surmounted with rather an elegant cupola. Sunday being a holiday for the people employed on the many tea plantations, it is taken advantage of for making bazaar, and on that day all the choicest goods are displayed by the enterprising tradesmen. These people nearly all squat on the ground with their goods beside and in front of them, and a curious collection it is; every variety of goods, including tin whistles, Crosse and Blackwell's pickles, jams and sardines, umbrellas, pots, pans, grid-irons, tooth-brushes, feeding-bottles, looking-glasses, cups, saucers and plates of the most ante-diluvian design and manufacture; tapes, cotton, needles and wooden spoons, Mrs. Allen's hair-dye, and Mrs. Winslow's soothing-syrup (I wonder if it is ever given to the native babies), in fact the most heterogeneous assortment of articles ever exhibited in any bazaar in the world. In addition, there are numberless articles of native manufacture; the thick, coarse striped woollen cloths, and soft silk (woven from the fibre that the peculiar worm which feeds on the castor-oil plant produces); Bhootea girdles, kukeries, &c., besides most uninviting vegetables, coarse tea and tobacco, goats, skinny sheep, beef of a colour that makes one shudder, poultry so attenuated that they look as if they had been raised for their bones only, rice, coarse grain in every variety, and ugly pigs.

The noise the vendors and purchasers make, chaffering, shouting, howling, singing, is something terrific. It is both interesting and amusing to watch the coolies and others as they flock to and fro, in incessant strings, some coming in to make their purchases, others returning home, the women with the useful hill bamboo basket slung to their backs, the men never without their kukeries stuck in their belts, laughing, joking, playing with each other, many of them more than half intoxicated with the drink they make from *murwah.**

A sturdy independent lot these people are, looking capable of holding their own with any one. They are, even in their dirt, picturesque: Limboos, Lepchas, Nepalese, Bhooteas, Cabulese, and stalwart Thibetans, who on their little hardy mountain ponies, dash along the road at a mad gallop; fine stalwart-looking fellows in spite of, or notwithstanding, their pig-tails. The Bhooteas are tall, the Lepchas and Limboos short and stunted, in fact there are to be seen representatives of every class and tribe in the district, as well as the poor plantation coolie. You meet both men and women of the better class. The richer Bhootea women look really handsome, their broad faces shining with good temper and mirth; they wear a circlet round the head which is very becoming; many of them are loaded both with gold and silver ornaments round their necks and in their ears; so heavy are the latter, that they actually weigh down the lobes of the ears. They usually wear massive silver girdles with appendages, not unlike a lady's chatelaine. One thing we cannot help remarking is their extreme rotundity of person, the middle-aged women being all of the

---

* *Murwah* is a millet extensively cultivated by the natives of the hills, it produces a small seed, which when fermented makes a mildly intoxicating drink, greatly favoured by them. The seed is put into what is called a *chonga*, a kind of bamboo bottle, water is poured in and left until the seed is well soaked, the liquor is then strained off, and drunk hot through a bamboo pipe, it is often flavoured with some pungent condiment, and the taste is something like the sweet wort used for brewing purposes in England; like beer, it is only intoxicating when taken in large quantities.

"Sairy Gamp" style. The poorer women, like their sisters at home, seem to have a full quiver of reproductions, for not only will there be seen two or three hanging from their mother's skirts, but often one or more (twins perhaps) strapped inside the inevitable bamboo basket, looking happy and contented, though we cannot endorse the opinion of the Hon'ble Emily Eden, as expressed in her diary, that "little native babies are much prettier than little English ditto."

CHAPTER VI.

ROADS AND EXCURSIONS.

THE roads in and about Darjeeling are those under the management of the Public Works Department, which are subdivided into Imperial and Provincial; those under the management of the District Roads Cess Committee; and those under the management of the Municipal Commissioners of Darjeeling. The total length of these roads is about 450 miles.

The Cart Road, which is an Imperial one, is now traversed by the Railway.

The following is a list of some of the principal roads near the Station of Darjeeling, and leading to different points in the interior of the District; with their distances:—

	Miles.
From the Chourasta to the Great Rungeet river, *viâ* Lebong and Badamtam	13
From the Chourasta round Birch Hill and back ...	5
From the Chourasta by the Auckland Road to Jore Bungalow	5
From the Chourasta to Mount Sinchul ...	6
From the Chourasta to the Victoria Waterfall ...	1½

	Miles.
From the Chourasta to the Teesta Bridge, *viâ* Rungaroon and Pashok	19
From the Chourasta to Toungloo, *viâ* Goompahar and Jor Pookri	31
From Toungloo to Sendukphoo	7
From Sendukphoo to Phaloot	13
From the Chourasta to the Lloyd Botanic Gardens...	1
From the Chourasta to the Jore Bungalow, *viâ* the Old Calcutta Road	4
From the Chourasta to the Barracks at Jellapahar...	2½
From the Chourasta to Rungaroon	6
From Teesta Bridge to Kalimpong	6
From Rungeet Cane Bridge to Junction with Teesta	7
From Junction to Teesta Bridge	4

All these roads are favourite ones with visitors who wish to see the best views of the District.

It would be well to warn travellers to come up to Darjeeling well provided with good warm woollen clothing, worsted socks, good stout boots and plenty of them, and good English saddlery, and to fully inspect the house they intend to occupy before engaging it, so as to be sure that it is not built over a spring or immediately under a heavy revetment; and to make sure that the walls are not damp, and that the drainage is in good order.

One of the most favourite excursions from Darjeeling is to the top of *Mount Sinchul*, as it is the nearest point from the station which affords a good view of Mount Everest, the highest mountain in the world. Everest is in Nepal, is distant about 80 miles as the crow flies, and is 29,000 feet high. The road from Jore Bungalow to Sinchul is always in good order, and is lined on both sides by primæval forest, with park-like clearings. The forest mainly consists of oak, magnolia and other large trees, mostly with epiphides of various species clinging round their trunks. Many beautiful ferns may be picked up along the road-side. The view from Sinchul is, probably, not to be surpassed. To the north is the station of Darjeeling, with its white villa residences clustering along the sides of the basin for a foreground, while in the background is the stupendous Snowy Range in all its glorious magnificence. Away to the N.-W. will be seen Mount Everest, appearing in the distance of the size and shape of a soldier's white helmet without the spike. Towards the south the plains of Bengal, spread out like a panorama, are to be seen stretching as far as the eye can reach. A more extensive view is obtainable by climbing Tiger Hill, the summit of which is nearly 1,000 feet above the level of the Sinchul parade ground. During the rainy season there is a good deal of lottery about being able to obtain a view from Sinchul, as the excursionist may often leave Darjeeling when the whole country round is bathed in the very brighest sunshine, while before he can get even half way to his destination the mists come surging up and around in dense masses, shutting the view in completely, and the traveller returns to Darjeeling a sadder, a wetter, and haply, a wiser man. The best plan for ensuring, as far as possible, a really good view from Mount Sinchul is to wait patiently until heavy rain has fallen for three or four days in succession, and then, if no rain is falling, a couple of hours before daybreak, to make a dash for it. The sunrise will amply,—indeed more than amply,—repay the early rising, and it is quite possible to be back in Darjeeling in time for a comfortable breakfast. From the close of the rains, about the middle of October, to the middle of December, and again from March to about the middle of May, splendid views can be relied on almost any and every day. Sunset from Sinchul is also most striking, the effects of the various lights on the Snowy Range being indescribably beautiful. For getting the full effect of a sunset from Sinchul, an evening when the setting of the sun and the rising of a nearly full moon nearly coincide, should be chosen.

Another pleasant excursion, in exactly the opposite direction, is from Darjeeling to the *Rungeet Cane Bridge*—distance 13 miles. Leaving the Chourasta, the road descends rapidly to the *Bhootea Bustee*, a collection of huts occupied mainly by Bhooteas, Limboos, and Lepchas, most of whom are porters, dandy-bearers, domestic servants, and dealers in curios; with their hangers-on of sorts. There is a large trade, and a very lucrative one too, done here in armlets, ornaments, praying wheels, skins, horns, Chinese and Thibetan crockery (a large proportion of it from Staffordshire), *kookeries*, *bans*, and all sorts of miscellaneous articles. The dealers are sharp hands at a bargain, and usually ask five times the proper value for their wares, and even when the vendors have apparently been beaten down to the lowest possible price, they go away with the "smile which is childlike and bland," and cheered with the inner consciousness that they have "sold" their customer. Here is a Buddhist *Goompah* which is worth seeing. There is no difficulty about obtaining admission, and the Lamas, who are a fat, cheery lot of old fellows, with not the least trace of asceticism about them are glad to shew visitors round the temple. Intending visitors should provide themselves with a good supply of Eau de Cologne, as the sacred atmosphere of the interior is a good deal removed from that of "Araby the Blest." Leaving the *Bhootea Bustee* the road runs along the eastern side of the Lebong spur, on a portion of the ridge of which the new barracks will ultimately be constructed, with the Minchu, Bannockburn and Ging Tea Plantations below on the right hand side. From the *Bustee* to the Badamtam Tea Plantation the road has been fairly level, but it now begins to descend rather rapidly in places. About the eighth mile from Darjeeling there is a very neat and comfortable rest bungalow, where either breakfast or tiffin can be partaken of; but the traveller must provide his own commissariat. The road then continues to descend rapidly through a virgin forest of sâl, pine and other trees, the undergrowth consisting of dense sub-tropical vegetation, and the air is almost alive with gorgeous butterflies and other insects. In time the right bank of the Runjeet is reached, and after crossing the Rungnoo (one of its affluents) by a substantial wooden bridge, the excursionist reaches the well-known cane bridge, or *Julunga.* The Runjeet rises in Independent Sikkim, and has its source at the foot of Kinchinjunga. This river from the point where the Rummun flows into it to its junction with the Teesta, forms the northern boundary of British Sikkim. The best time to see this river in all its grandeur is during the rains, when it is full of water, but it is well worth seeing at any period of the year, as it is really a noble river, and during the cold season is perfectly limpid. The river is full of fish, and "takes" of gigantic *mahaseer* have been known; but, somehow, the Indian carp in this river is either too well-fed or too cunning to respond readily to the "voice of the charmer" with a fishing rod in his hand, and the brethren of the angle who have tried to circumvent him, have generally returned home with empty baskets. The *mahaseer* has been occasionally accounted for with a spoon-bait, and this is really the only one that will take a "rise" out of him. Since a permanent bridge has been constructed across the Teesta, the Julunga across the Runjeet at this point is the most important in the Darjeeling District. As a good sample of primitive bridge-making alone, it is worth seeing. The bridge is a suspension one, constructed entirely of cane, with a bamboo footway. Nervous people often hesitate about crossing this apparently flimsy structure, swinging as it does in mid air from one bank to the other of a broad, deep and rapid river; but there is absolutely no danger whatever, the bridge, in spite of the appearances against it, is perfectly safe. Major Sherwill gives a technical description of the construction of these Julungas, which will probably be of interest to the reader. It is as follows:—

"The main chains supporting the bridge are composed of five rattan canes each; the sides are of split cane hanging from each main chain as loops, two feetap art, and two feet deep. Into these loops the platform is laid, composed of three bamboos, the size of a man's arm, laid side by side, the section of the bridge resembling the letter V, in the angle or base of which the traveller finds footing. Outriggers, to prevent the main chains being brought together with the weight of the passenger, are placed at every ten or twelve feet in the following manner: under the platform and parallel to the stream strong bamboos are passed, and from their extremities to the main chain (of cane) split rattan ropes are firmly tied. This prevents the hanging loop or bridge from shutting up and choking the passenger. The piers of these bridges (for there are several of them) are generally two convenient trees, through whose branches the main chains are passed, and pegged into the ground of the opposite side."

From here the excursionist has his choice of returning to Darjeeling by the way he came, or of proceeding along the right bank of the Runjeet to its junction with the Teesta, and thence to the new Iron Suspension Bridge. His course will entirely depend on the arrangements he has made, before leaving Darjeeling, as to coolies, supplies, &c. Supposing the traveller to have decided to make an excursion of two clear days' duration, he will send his bedding, provisions, and other impedimenta, on to the Pashok rest-house early the same morning that he starts for the Runjeet, having first, of course, obtained permission from the Executive Engineer to occupy the bungalow at Pashok. Starting from Darjeeling in good time in the morning after a really substantial *chota hazaree*, he will reach the Runjeet with a good healthy appetite for breakfast, at an hour which will depend entirely on whether he travels fast or slow. Having admired the scenery in the gorge of the river, while digesting his meal, and mayhap having smoked the contemplative pipe and having, "just for the name of the thing," crossed into Independent Sikkim either by the Cane Bridge or on a "dug-out" at the ferry, he will again take horse and ride to the "Junction," a distance of between six and seven miles, along a really capital level road, skirting the Runjeet the whole way.

There are constantly succeeding peeps of the most splendidly varied scenery along this road—river, forest, and mountain; and if the traveller can at all appreciate the beauties of nature, he will constantly draw bridle and admire the lovely scenery. The Junction of the Teesta and the Runjeet is strikingly and wonderfully beautiful. Tommy Moore never was in India, and even if he had been, he could never have done justice to this "Meeting of the Waters," and we will not attempt it. All we can say to visitors to Darjeeling is, go and see the place yourselves, and if you do not thank us for the advice, you are indeed blind. There is a marked and striking difference in colour between the water of these two rivers, and for some distance below the actual junction of the two, the waters of each retains each its distinctive character. The water of the Teesta is sea-green, somewhat tinged, and several degrees lower in temperature than that of the Runjeet, while the latter is of a dark greenish blue, and perfectly transparent. Following the right bank of the Teesta for about four miles, along a good level road, the traveller reaches the recently constructed Iron Suspension Bridge. This has taken the place of the old primitive *Julunga*, and is the route taken by most of the trade between Darjeeling, Thibet, and Bhootan. The Bridge is a light looking, though substantial, structure, and reflects much credit on both the D. P. W. and the Contractors, Messrs. Burn & Co. of Calcutta. From the Bridge to the Inspection Bungalow is a steady pull of about three miles up the hill. There the traveller can rest for the night and proceed next morning to Darjeeling, a distance of about fifteen miles, through the forest on the Tukolah ridge and under Sinchul. The road is really good all the way, and the forest scenery very striking. The traveller can reverse this itinerary if it seems good to him. During the rains excursionists would be on the safe side if they were to take a few grains of quinine morning and evening, and they should bear in mind on no account to start in the morning, without having first partaken of a really substantial *chota hazaree.* Above all things, travellers should carefully eschew bathing in either the Runjeet or the Teesta. If they neglect this warning, they must not be surprised if their indiscretion is followed by an attack of congestion of the liver, or intermittent fever, or both.

Another very pleasant excursion from Darjeeling, is to the *Rungaroon Botanic Garden*—distance 6 miles. The excursionist can either go by the old Calcutta Road, or over Jellapahar. When the Saddle is reached, the road turns sharply to the left for a distance of a little over 2 miles, where the bridle path down to the Gardens is reached. The turning cannot be mistaken, as there is a sign post at the side of the road. After a short descent the Forest bungalow is reached. This is always available for picnics, if permission to use it is asked for beforehand.

The experimental *Botanical Garden* was founded at Rungaroon by order of Sir Richard Temple, then Lieutenant-Governor of Bengal.. The area of which is above 75 acres, of which rather more than twenty-six acres is under forest, the gardens and nurseries have been laid out, and bungalows built. The garden is first and foremost a Botanical one. Plants of all species—epiphytes, orchids, gingers, &c., that will grow at the elevation of Rungaroon are collected and attached to the trees, so as to make a representative piece of virgin forest, and vacant spaces have been filled with species indigenous to Nepal, Sikkim, or Bhootan. In short, the garden is devoted to such indigenous plants as are not likely to thrive in the moisture and more shady forest sections, a third being reserved for exotic plants of botanical interest and suited to the climate and elevation.

More attention is given to the growth of indigenous plants than to that of exotics. Every possible flowering plant, growing naturally in these districts between 8,000 feet and 9,000 feet, is considered worthy of being tried, either in the cleared, or forest section of the garden.

As regards the exotic garden, the selection of plants is made with the idea of representing Natural Orders which are not abundant, or which do not occur at all in the mountainous parts of India. Many of the Australian *Protcaceæ* and of the European and American *Coniferæ* and *Capuliferæ* have been some time planted, the first and last of these species are growing fairly, the *Coniferæ* order, that is, the trees most peculiar to mountain regions,—cedars, firs, pines, larches, spruces, cypresses, &c., are flourishing. It is a remarkable fact that these trees are not indigenous in the hills round Darjeeling. But the selection of plants grown in the exotic garden will have to be worked out by the help of experience as to what kind of plants are likely to thrive in a wet climate such as that of Sikkim. The situation of the garden is excellent; it is on the slope at the lower edge of the forest which clothes the Sinchul′ mountain and somewhat lower than Darjeeling, its altitude being about 6,000 feet; it has an excellent soil, and is well watered most months of the year by running streams.

Another pleasant, but more ambitious, expedition is to *Phaloot* on the Singalila Range. This immense spur runs from Kinchinjunga to the plains of India, a distance of sixty miles, and during the greater portion of its course forms the boundary between Eastern Nepal and Sikkim. The road runs through the Goompahar Forest, and is in very fair order to Tongloo. At the 8th mile from Darjeeling one of the natural curiosities of the district may be observed. It is an enormous rock on the top of the ridge, from the summit of which a magnificent view of Darjeeling and the Snowy Range on one side, and of the plains of Bengal on the other, is to be obtained. An easy zig-zag path leads to the summit of the rock, which is situated on the right hand side of the road. Near the 9th mile is a rest-house, but it is better to push on to that at Jor Pookri—13 miles from Darjeeling—and to breakfast there, thus leaving plenty of time for the journey to Tongloo, 31 miles. The distance of this mountain, which is 10,074 feet high, is only 11 miles in a straight line from Darjeeling; but it must be remembered that the road traverses two sides of a triangle. The best and most comfortable plan is to sleep at Tongloo, so as to be fresh for an early start in the morning. From Tongloo to Sendukphoo the distance is 7 miles over a fairly good road, although in places it is rather trying for nervous people. Sendukphoo is 11,929 feet high, and from it there is a glorious view of the Nepaulese Snowy Range, including peaks west of the Arun river, Chumglang (22,215 feet), Chumglang No. 2, (24,020 feet), Everest (29,002 feet), Everest No. 2 (27,799 feet). From Sendukphoo to Phaloot the distance is 13 miles, and the traveller can put up here for the night or return to Sendukphoo. There is a newly built rest bungalow here. Phaloot is 11,811 feet high, and 19 miles distant from Darjeeling in a straight line. Sunset and sunrise from any of these points are probably unsurpassable. The trip is a somewhat arduous and expensive one, but the scenery will amply repay both cost and trouble. A small army of coolies will have to be engaged, as only bedsteads, chairs and tables are provided in the rest bungalows, so that absolutely everything needed has to be brought from Darjeeling. The baggage coolies should be sent on towards Tongloo the day before a start is made, as if this precaution is not attended to, it is probable that they will not put in an appearance until late at night, and the traveller will be left hungry and shivering for many weary hours at Tongloo. Lots of wraps and warm clothing are essential for comfort in this trip, as it is bitterly cold on the ridge at night. Application for permission to use the rest bungalows should be made to the Deputy Commissioner of Darjeeling several days beforehand. The charge is one rupee for each person occupying them for a night. The best times for undertaking this expedition are from the middle of October to the middle of November, and from the middle of March to the middle of May, as during these periods of the year the sky is almost cloudless. Towards the end of March and the beginning of April, the Rhododendron Forest at Tongloo and Sendukphoo is one blaze of various colours.

Another excursion from Darjeeling is to the *Jeylup Pass*. This is the lowest pass in the range which divides Sikkim from Thibet. It is only 11,000 feet high, and is passable all the year round. The road to the Teesta Bridge has been already described. Crossing the Teesta, an ascent of some miles brings the traveller to the sub-divisional station of

Kalimpong, where there are a Forest Officer and a Presbyterian missionary. From thence five easy marches bring the traveller to the foot of the Pass, the road nearly all the way being passable for ponies. It is a long and trying climb to the summit, but once that point has been reached, there is a wonderful view of Thibet available. The town of Chombi in Thibet is about 20 miles from this point. The Rajah of Sikkim lives at Chombi during a portion of the year. It will be necessary to take tents, and provisions of all kinds for self and coolies, as there are no houses to be met with between the third march from Kalimpong and the foot of the Pass. It hardly needs mentioning that Europeans are not allowed to cross into Thibet. The guard has quarters at Chombi, but somehow the news leaks out that a European is on his way to the Pass, and he almost invariably finds the guard waiting his arrival, and he is firmly but respectfully told that there is "no thoroughfare." People with any tendency to weakness of the heart or lungs, should on no account attempt the ascent to the Pass.

There are many trips, pleasant and easy enough, which may be undertaken in Independent Sikkim, such as to the great Lamissary of Pemianchi, to Toomlong, the capital of the country, and other places. There is absolutely no shooting to be had without undergoing very great fatigue; and nine days out of ten would be blank for the sportsman under any circumstances. A good walker would thoroughly tire of a week or ten days' tour in Independent Sikkim. A light tent, tinned provisions, tea, &c., should be brought from Darjeeling. Fowls, rice, and Indian corn are procurable at every village, so that it would not be necessary to burden one's self with food for coolies, and indeed it is not necessary to take many of them, who are, if at all numerous, a perfect plague to the traveller. The people are frank, hospitable, obliging, and fond of Europeans. They will be described fully in another chapter.

There are many delightful walks and rides in and about Darjeeling, among which may be mentioned the walks round Birch Hill, along the Auckland Road to the Jore Bungalow and back, either over the Jella-pahar or along the old Calcutta Road; to the Victoria Waterfall, including a visit to the Burdwan Rajah's Palace; &c., &c. In fact in whatever direction the traveller goes he will find on all sides something to amuse and interest him. During the rains he should never be far away from his waterproof, as the showers come down in the most unexpected way. The pedestrian should also make a point of wearing good, stout, clump-soled boots. A drenching never hurts if care is taken to change the clothes immediately on returning home.

CHAPTER VII.

TRADE—TEA AND CINCHONA CULTIVATION.

A VERY brisk trade is carried on between Darjeeling, Sikkim, Bhootan, and Thibet. During the financial year 1880-1 the imports from Sikkim were valued at Rs. 1,67,960, and the exports at Rs. 80,898. During the same period the imports from Bhootan were valued at Rs. 2,43,922, and the exports at Rs. 1,96,947. The principal articles imported from Sikkim were food grains, ponies, cattle, ghee, and salt. The principal exports to Sikkim were European piece goods, salt, and tobacco. The principal articles of import from Bhootan were woollen goods, ponies, and madder (a red, fast dye) locally known as *maujit.* The principal articles of export were European piece goods, tobacco, betelnuts, and rice. Most of the sturdy little ponies one sees in and about Darjeeling have been imported through Bhootan and Sikkim from Thibet. There is also a large trade in chiretta, and enormous numbers of oranges pass through Darjeeling in the cold weather on their way from Independent Sikkim to the plains.

TEA cultivation and manufacture is the most important industry in British Sikkim, and employs a large number of Europeans as well as a host of native tea-makers and coolies. In fact it may be safely asserted that the European tea planter has done more to develop the natural resources of this beautiful country within a short space of years than could be accomplished in centuries without his aid, as the following figures will prove conclusively.

Comparative Table of Tea Operations from the year 1866 to 1880-81.

Years.	Number of gardens.	Extent of land under cultivation in acres.	Outturn of tea in lbs.	Number of Labourers employed.
1866	39	16,392	433,715	Not known.
1868	44	10,067	851,549	6,859
1870	56	11,046	1,689,186	8,347
1872	74	14,503	2,938,626	12,361
1874	113	18,881	3,927,911	19,424
1880	155	28,367	5,160,314	Not accurately known. Cannot be less than 28,000
1882	154	25,105	6,596,456	Ditto.

Of the labourers employed on the tea estates fully 99 per cent. are immigrants from Nepaul, or their descendants who have settled down permanently in the district. The first tea-seeds in this district were planted in his garden at Beerdwood by the late Dr. Campbell, then Superintendent of Darjeeling. The seeds were of the China variety, and the older parts of the older gardens were planted with China seed. The seed is supposed to have been obtained from Kumaon. Attempts were made to introduce tea cultivation into Darjeeling some time previously to 1853, when two or three small gardens existed, but the real date of the commencement of the industry may be taken at 1856-57. The earlier planters had to grope about a good deal in the dark owing to want of practical experience, they consequently made many serious mistakes, and their ventures did not meet with success. There was also in the "good old days" a good deal of sharp practice, if not knavery, in the sale of gardens to enthusiastic and unsuspecting purchasers. Mr. A. wanted money, he had a large grant of land, he sowed it broadcast with tea-seed, and then he waited patiently for a spider to walk into his net. The spider came in time, and Mr. A. sold his land to Mr. B. as being so many acres of land under tea,—probably exaggerating the actual area of the land, as in those days there was no means of checking statements of this kind; and when the bargain was concluded, Mr. B. found that the land represented to him as being several hundred acres planted with tea, really meant so many acres with some couple of hundred plants per acre. In those days it was a common saying "it pays to plant tea, but it does not pay to make it." The meaning of which is, that a good profit was to be made by planting out tea in the way described above, and then selling it to a greenhorn before the time the bushes came into bearing. This dishonesty was one of the factors in the crash of 1865-66. Since then people have learned from dearly bought experience, and the last twelve years have been a period of steadily increasing prosperity.

The following is a brief description of tea cultivation. Having obtained a suitable block of land, if possible with water-power available, and not too far off a main road, and arrangements having been made for an adequate supply of good seed (Assam hybrid for choice), and a sufficient supply of labour, operations commence about the middle of October. The first thing to be done is to clear the land intended for planting. This is done by burning the undergrowth when it is sufficiently dry to take light freely. The heavy timber (if any) is singed and left standing for the present, or felled at once. The jungle having been burned, the coolies are set to work to grub out roots, and afterwards to hoe the entire surface to be planted to a depth of from one-and-a-half to two feet. Roads are then lined out and the land is staked off with bamboo stakes at a distance of from three to four feet apart, shewing where the tea plants are to be. Holes of 18 inches deep by one foot in diameter are next dug at each of the stakes, in which the surface soil is to be placed. This work is usually finished by the end of November. One or two seeds are now planted in the holes (although some people plant as many as three or four), and are pushed down to the depth of an inch. They are then covered over with loose soil. "Nurseries" are formed at the same time at places where irrigation is possible, and filled with seed closely planted. These "nurseries" are intended as a reserve, from which young plants can be removed during the rainy season to fill up any vacancies that may be caused by any of the seed at stake not having germinated. The garden having been planted, the next thing to do is to erect some permanent buildings, such as a bungalow for the manager, with the necessary out-buildings and houses for the coolies. All that now remains to be done is to keep the planted land clear of weeds, and to fill in vacancies with transplants from the "nurseries" during the rainy season.

In the third year all the plants should be from 2 feet 6 inches to 4 or 5 feet high, according to the variety of seed sown. The China is the slowest and the Assam the quickest grower. They are then pruned down to about 20 inches from the ground, in order to promote the growth of new wood and tender shoots. Pruning is done between November and February, when the sap is down, and this is an operation requiring great care and attention from all concerned. About a month or six weeks after pruning, according to weather, elevation and aspect, the new shoots are on an average from 6 to 8 inches long, and can now be picked; and from this period throughout the rains successive "flushes," *i.e.*, new shoots, make their appearance at intervals varying from fifteen to twenty days, according to soil, weather, elevation and system of pruning adopted. The tea plant is said to "flush" when it throws out new shoots and leaves. A well-cultivated garden planted with a good *jât* of plant not too far apart, should give in its 5th or 6th year about 240 lbs. of manufactured tea per acre; which is reckoned as being equivalent to 240 lbs. of green leaf brought into the factory. The outturn increases steadily until the twelfth year, when the bush has arrived at maturity. The yield will then be about 320 lbs. an acre. It is a fallacy to suppose that a tea plant will give a larger crop than this steadily year after year. It is true that as much as from 700 to 900 lbs. an acre have been reached, but the results to the planters have been disastrous in every case. The tea made has been coarse, has consequently sold for prices which hardly paid for manufacture, and the trees have required many years of careful nursing to recover from such rough treatment.

Pruning is now steadily and systematically carried on during the cold weather, and the gardens, as a rule, are deep hoed twice or oftener during the rains.

As soon as the flush is in a sufficiently advanced stage, as many women and children as are needed are employed to take it off the bushes before it has time to get hard, as the younger and more succulent the leaf, the better will be the tea manufactured from it. The principle in plucking is to leave the bud at the axis of the leaf down to which the shoot is plucked intact, as from this axis the next "flush" starts. Some authorities name the leaves as follows from the teas they would make, supposing six leaves were plucked;—1, Flowery Pekoe; 2, Orange Pekoe; 3, Orange Pekoe; 4, Souchong; 5, Congou; or mixed together—1, 2, 3, Pekoe; 1, 2, 3, 4, 5, Pekoe Souchong. If No. 6 be taken into account it would make a coarse kind of Bohea. This, so far as the Darjeeling district is concerned, is extremely misleading. Flowery and Orange Pekoes are almost never manufactured, and the following is the correct classification;—1, Pekoe; 2, Souchong; 3, Broken Pekoe; 4, Pekoe Fannings; 5, Souchong; 6, Broken Tea.

At 5 o'clock in the evening the factory gong rings and the pluckers hasten in with their baskets of leaf, which is carefully weighed and examined. It is then spread on the floor of the withering loft in a thin layer, and on the floor of the factory, if there be not room for it above, in order to allow the leaf to wither. This process takes longer or shorter according to temperature. The best tests by which it is known whether the leaf is sufficiently withered, are the following. Fresh leaf gathered in the hand and held near the ear gives a crackling sound, but no sound should be heard from properly withered leaf. The stalk of withered leaf will bend double without breaking; this the fresh stalk will not do. If the leaf is brought dry to the factory, the leaf is usually withered by early morning.

When sufficiently withered a variable quantity, according to the capacity of the rolling machines now so universally used, and which are driven either by steam or water-power, is put into the machine and rolled until the operation has been completed. This takes longer or shorter according to whether the leaf is hard or soft. The leaf is then taken out of the machine and formed into balls, although some people give a light hand rolling afterwards, as this is supposed to give a better "twist" to the leaf. The balls are then allowed to stand until fermentation sets in. This is the most delicate and important of all the stages of tea-making, as on it depends the future quality of the tea. The fermentation should be stopped at the right moment, and it needs a sharp and experienced eye to tell when the proper amount of fermentation has been arrived at. As a rule the inside of the ball of leaf should be of the colour of a new saddle. The fermented leaf is then spread on fine meshed wire trays and placed over a charcoal fire, or in one of the new drying machines which are now coming into general use, where it is shaken up and re-dried several times until it is thoroughly dry and crisp. The manufacture is now complete; the leaf brought into the factory has become tea. The tea is now left to cool. The next process is to sift the tea into its separate qualities. For this purpose sieves of different meshes are used, and this is done either by women or in a sifting machine. The best quality of tea falls through the finer meshes, while the coarser remains in the sieve. This latter is then put on a coarser sieve, and so on until nothing remains but the red, hard, unrolled tea. The tea is then re-heated, and is closely packed in wooden boxes lined with sheet lead. The tea is now ready to send to market. Gteen tea is never made in this district.

There is every prospect now that Indian Tea has becomc so well known in both the home and foreign markets, and that scientific planting and manufacture have becn universally adopted, in addition to the vast improvements arrived at in the machinery of late years, that the tea industry in these hills is certain to continue in a flourishing condition.

A tea plantation is well worthy of a visit, especially during the manufacturing season, when the different processes briefly sketched above can be seen in operation. The plantations are models of neatness and order, and the planters are always willing to explain each process and the reason for it to visitors. The Nepaulese coolies, too, are very interesting. In spite of a pretty liberal coating of dirt, some of the women are good-looking, and men and women alike are a happy-go-lucky lot, cheerful and in good condition. In fact just the reverse of the Bengali laborers in every respect. They are well paid and well housed, and each family has its little patch of cultivation rent-free, on which maize and muarwa (a sort of small millet) are grown. That they are better off on the tea gardens, than in their own country is proved by their immigrating into Sikkim and settling down there in such numbers.

CINCHONA cultivation and the manufacture of the celebrated Alkaloid Febrifuge is the next most important industry carried on in this district. The plantations are situated at Rungbee and Mongpoo, at which latter place the factories are, in the valley of the Riang, and at Sittong in the valley of the Teesta. The road to Rungbee branches off at the 3rd mile from the Jore Bungalow on the Tukodah road. From the turning the ride is a longish one, but it is certainly far from being a weary one, as the forest scenery along it is certainly the finest now remaining in this district.

Like tea, there was a good deal of groping about in the dark at the outset of this industry. In 1862 some cases containing a number of plants and seedlings were sent up from Calcutta and were 15 days or more on the road. Many of the plants died *en route.* The cases were then sent to Senchul of all places in the world, because some wiseacre concluded that as cinchona grew and flourished on the higher slopes of the equatorial Andes, Senchul must be *the* place for them. It is needless to say that dearly bought experience proved that the climate was utterly unsuitable; so in time they were moved to Lebong. This place also proving unfit for the plants, they were moved to Rungaroon, but their migrations were now almost at an end, as finally an enormous block of land bounded on the north by the Riang river and on the east by the Teesta was taken up as a suitable place for the new industry. That the selection was a judicious one has been amply proved by experience. The financial results of the Cinchona plantations, as proved by the unerring test of figures, have exceeded the wildest dreams of the most enthusiastic advocate.

In 1862 there were 311 plants and 1,300 seedling on the Government Cinchona Plantations. In 1875 there were about 2,000 acres of Government Plantation, in which the trees were from 4 to 30 feet high, according to their age. The total number of trees, (excluding plants in the nurseries) put out between 1864 and the 31st March, 1875, amounted to 3,285,592. The number of trees of all kinds on the plantations at the end of the financial year 1882 was 859,323. During that year the produce of the plantations was 34,570lbs. of dry bark, and 10,876lbs. of febrifuge were disposed of. The total revenue of the plantations was Rs. 2,72,214, with a net profit of Rs. 1,30,338, representing a return at the rate of 13 per cent. on the capital. In addition a sum of probably nearly five lakhs of rupees was saved to Government, by the substitution of febrifuge for quinine in the public institutions of the country. At the end of the year there were 858,323 quinine giving trees on the plantations, namely, *Calisaya* (including *ledgeriana*) 566,695, and hybrids 291,628. There was no addition during the year to the alkaloid giving trees, *succirubra*, during the year, as the number at present on the plantation 3,873,285 was considered to meet all present demand for febrifuge.

Thus in twenty years, from a very small beginning, a splendidly successful enterprise has been established; splendid not only financially, but splendid on humanitarian grounds besides, as it has put an efficient febrifuge within the reach of the very poorest native of Bengal. Many years ago an attempt was made to manufacture quinine on the spot, but like most first efforts it turned out a failure. The Government, although naturally discouraged, did not give up the effort to manufacture a cheap antiperiodic on the spot, instead of being obliged to incur the needless expense of sending the bark home to be worked up into quinine there, and then be re-imported in that form. After numerous experiments, Mr. Wood succeeded in obtaining an alkaloid from the Government bark. There was furious opposition on the part of a portion of the "faculty" to the introduction of this alkaloid into the public institutions as a substitute for quinine, and reams of paper were wasted in exhaustive reports, trying to prove that the alkaloid was worse than useless. However, time proved that the opposition were entirely in the wrong, and it is now acknowledged that the febrifuge is quite as useful as quinine in most cases of intermittent fever. When Mr. Wood left India, Mr. Gamsmie took over the direction of the factory, and has succeeded in improving the quality of the amorphous alkaloid, as well as in producing an alkaloid little inferior in appearance and solubility to sulphate of quinine, while it is fully equal to it in efficacy.

The mode of extracting the febrifuge from the bark is roughly as follows:—The bark is first reduced to a rough powder, the powder is then soaked in enough dilute muriatic acid to make it thoroughly moist. After soaking for a variable period, and stirring the mass occasionally, the mass is then put into an apparatus, and is allowed to percolate with the dilute muriatic acid, until the solution which drops through is nearly destitute of a bitter taste. A solution of caustic soda is then added to the liquor and it is well stirred. The resulting precipitate is then allowed to subside gradually, the supernatant liquor is then drawn off, the precipitate is thoroughly washed with cold water until the washings cease to have colour. The precipitate with some more water is then heated and dilute sulphuric acid added gradually until nearly all the precipitate has been dissolved, and a neutral liquid has been obtained. The liquid is then concentrated until a film begins to form. Many details are omitted in this description for obvious reasons, but this is an outline of the various processes through which the bark has to pass before being converted into alkaloid or febrifuge.

Under this heading FOREST CONSERVANCY may be appropriately introduced, because the reboissement of these hills already far too much denuded, as well as the preservation of the existing forest and the supply of fuel and timber, is a most important industry in this district. The Forest Reserves in this district are the Darjeeling, Kurseong, and Teesta Divisions. The estimated area of the first is 24,288 acres, of the second 57,392 acres, and of the third 161,255 acres. These divisions are again subdivided into blocks of various sizes. The forests extend from the Sâl Forest of the plains, to the region of oaks and pines, or from an elevation of 300 to 10,000 feet above the sea-level. A list of the trees growing between these elevations will be found at pp. 16 and 17 *ante*. The work of planting out young trees at the various elevations suitable to the growth of the various species is being carried out vigorously and systematically, while nurseries have been formed in different parts of the reserves, and efficient measures have been taken for the protection of the existing forests from fires, by preventing *jhuming*, and setting apart places where travellers may light their cooking fires with safety to the forest. The supply of wood fuel to the station of Darjeeling, is partly carried on by the Forest Department, and partly by native contractors. The prevailing rates for firewood are Rs 25 per 100 maunds, and for charcoal R 1 per maund; these rates do not include carriage to the purchaser's house, which is charged for according to the distance the fuel has to be carried previous to delivery. Fuel is a heavy item in the monthly household expenditure, but there is no help for it at present, and people can only grumble and put up with it. There is, however, every prospect of the Railway being able before long to deliver coal and coke at Darjeeling, at less rates in proportion than those at present obtaining for firewood and charcoal.

CHAPTER VIII.

THE HILL TRIBES OF SIKKIM AND ITS VICINITY AND THE INHABITANTS OF THE DARJEELING TERAI.

THE native inhabitants of the hill portions of Sikkim may be roughly divided into, 1, Nepalese, 2, Lepchas, 3, Bhooteas.

The LEPCHAS may be regarded as the aborigines of the hill portion of Sikkim, although they have a tradition that at some remote period, they migrated across the snows into this country. At all events they were the first race found in Sikkim, so far as can be ascertained. To all frequenters of Darjeeling this race must be very familiar. They undertake all sorts of odd jobs, and are not averse to undertake domestic service occasionally, and if fairly treated will remain in the same family for years. They have no objection to turning their hands to any kind of indoor work, and as they are generally intelligent and easily trained, they in time become valuable domestic servants. The women are capital children's servants. Their features are of a distinctly Mongolian type, their faces being broad and flat, their eyes oblique, with high cheek bones. They have broad chests, very well developed calves to their legs, and fairly muscular arms, but in spite of this, they are, as a rule, decidedly effeminate looking. This may be owing to their short stature (rarely exceeding 5 ft. 2 in. or 5 ft. 4 in. in height) small hands and feet and almost hairless faces; the men have a small down of hair on the upper lip. Their hair is coarse and coal black, and grows long and thick, and the men plait it into *one* tail, while the women wear *two*. This is often the only means a new-comer has of distinguishing a man from a woman at little distance. This race is gradually, but surely, dying out in British Sikkim, and probably in Independent Sikkim also, and before many generations are past, the pure-blooded Lepcha will be as extinct as the Dodo. This is in a great measure due to the increase of regular cultivation of late years, and to the strict conservation of the forests by the Forest Department. They have not a word for plough in their language, and follow the nomadic mode of raising crops by *jhum* cultivation. This consists in selecting a patch of virgin soil, clearing it of forest and jungle, and scraping up the surface with the rudest agricultural implements. The productive powers of the cleared land become exhausted in three or four years, when it is abandoned and a new site chosen, where the same operation is repeated, and so on *ad infinitum*. It is obvious that with this system of cultivation, it would require a large tract of land to support even a moderate sized family. The Lepchas have no caste distinctions, but they speak of themselves as belonging to nine septs or clans; 1, Barphung Phucho; 2, Adeng Phucho; 3, Tharjoph Phucho; 4, Singrang; 5, Singut; 6, Tingel;

7, Luksom; 8, Tiren; and 9, Sangine. These all eat together and intermarry, but they talk of one clan being higher than another. The Lepchas have a tradition of the flood, during which a couple escaped to the top of Teendong, a mountain in Independent Sikkim not far from Darjeeling. Originally the Lepchas appear to have had no religion in the ordinary acceptation of the word. They acknowledge the existence of good and evil spirits. They pay no heed to the good spirits, "why should we," they say, "the good spirits do us no harm; the evil spirits who dwell in every rock, grove, and mountain, are constantly at work, and to them we must pray, for they hurt us." Every tribe has a priest-doctor, who neither knows nor attempts to practise the healing art, but whose chief business is to cast out the devils which are supposed to cause all human ailments. In fact he is an exorcist, pure and simple. These men are called *Bizwas*. The Lepchas respect the Bhuddist Lamas as holy men, and some of them profess a modified form of Bhuddism. They burn or bury their dead indifferently. Morally they are far superior to their neighbours, the Bhooteas and Thibetians. Polygamy is unknown and polyandry very rare. In their relations with each other and with Europeans they are frank, open, and used to be strictly honest in all their dealings; but it is to be feared that their contact in Darjeeling with the knavish Bengalees has corrupted them to some extent, but in his native wilds in Independent Sikkim he still preserves his good qualities intact, and it is only there that the Lepcha, pure and simple, is to be found now-a-days. Although a mountaineer, the Lepcha is an arrant coward, but he is a born naturalist and hunter, and has a name for every tree, shrub, animal, bird and insect to be found in Sikkim. His personal cleanliness troubles him very little. Though fond of a dip in any stream he may come across, he rarely washes himself, in our acceptation of the word, and is consequently not a pleasant neighbour in a hot valley, when he is to windward. They are very fond of a sort of quoits, at which game they play with pieces of slate, and are very expert. Their dress is distinctly graceful, consisting of a robe of striped blue and white cloth woven by the women in a very primitive loom ; this is crossed over the breast and back, leaving the arms free, and descending to the calf of the leg ; it is gathered in at the waist with an ornamented girdle. In winter they wear a long woollen upper garment with long loose sleeves. The dress of the women is very similar to that of the men, with the addition of a sort of bed gown over it, the material of which is got from the cocoons of a kind of caterpillar, which feeds on the leaves of a variety of nettle very common in this district, as any person who has been stung by it will have cause to remember. We have known the sting penetrate through a pair of cord riding brushes, and the pain caused by the sting is very far from being a joke for several hours after. The young tender tops of all the nettle tribe are used as food by the Lepchas. They make it into a sort of curry, and almost any day near Lepcha settlements the women may be seen going about amongst the nettles armed with a pair of pincers with which they remove the tops.

The Lepchas are gross-feeders, inordinately fond of Homeric meals of pork, and they eat the carcasses of cattle which have died of disease. Indeed, so fond are they of this latter savory (?) morsel that during an epidemic of cattle disease it is extremely difficult to prevent them from digging up, and eating the bodies which have been buried even so long as three days. They are very fond too of strong drink when they can get it. Their chief drink, however, is *murwa*, which is somewhat like exceedingly small table beer. This is made by pouring boiling water on the millet in a bamboo *chonga*, allowing it to cool a little and sucking the infusion through a bamboo tube. This when cleanly made is very refreshing, and is certainly non-intoxicant. The seeds are then given to the pigs and cattle who like and thrive on them. The Lepchas are also very fond of tea. They seem to prefer English made tea, when they can get it, and drink it as we do with milk and sugar. They also drink large quantities of the brick tea manufactured in China for the Thibet market. This they prepare in the following manner. A sufficient quantity of the brick having been broken off, it is put into a *chonga*, and some boiling water poured over it, butter and salt added, the whole is then churned up together, and the semi-solid liquid (if such a word can be coined) is poured into little cups, turned from knots of the maple and other trees, and drunk warm. We tried this mixture once, and it certainly was not exactly nauseous. Probably our palate was not properly educated; at all events the first experiment was also the last.

The marriage customs of the Lepchas are somewhat singular. The bridegroom has to purchase the bride. If the ardent lover have not sufficient either in coin or in kind to meet the demands of the parents, he pays what he can and goes through a form of preliminary marriage ceremony, which is considered perfectly binding on both sides. The bridegroom is not allowed to set up house-keeping for himself until the whole of the dowry is paid, so he consequently lives with his parents-in-law until the whole of the purchase-money has been paid up, it may be several years after, when a second marriage ceremony is gone through, and the husband is allowed to take his wife away with him. The conjugal relations of the Lepchas are singularly pure, unfaithfulness being very rare indeed. The besetting sin of the Lepcha is indolence. He will do nothing if he can avoid it. Still with all their faults, the Lepchas are by far the most pleasing, frank and honest race to be found in Sikkim. Those who know them best and are most alive to their faults like them best, because their sterling good qualities more than counterbalance their bad ones. It is a matter of sincere regret that this interesting race should be dying out fast, as is undoubtedly the case. Colonel Mainwaring published a grammar of the Lepcha language some few years ago, and has been at work on a dictionary during an indefinite period. Probably before the latter has issued from the press the last of the Lepchas will have passed away.

The NEPALESE form over 65 per cent. of the population of the Darjeeling hills, and they are immigrating in yearly increasing numbers. Independent Sikkim is also being rapidly populated by them. The Nepalese as seen in the Darjeeling District are divided iuto almost innumerable tribes or clans (improperly called castes). They are all immigrants from Nepal, and probably when we took possession of British Sikkim, there were hardly two hundred Nepalese of pure descent in the territory. Of course the

Limboos (whom we class under this head for convenience), were tolerably numerous, as they are a cross between the Lepcha and the Nepalese, and inhabit Sikkim and Eastern Nepal indifferently. The Nepalese are a pushing, thriving, prolific race. They are excellent cultivators, and when the slope of the land will allow of it they invariably use ploughs if they can afford a pair of bullocks, and if the land they occupy is sufficiently large. They find ready and well paid employment on the tea gardens, and many of them are engaged in trade. They are also largely employed as domestic servants, syces, leaf-cutters, &c. It is impossible to enumerate and describe all the clans in a moderate space even. The Murmis are the most numerous in this district, and next in order the Limboos, the Gunmugs, the Magars, the Kambas, the Ghartis, and the Nawars. These last were the original inhabitants of the Valley of Khatmandu, and were driven out by the Goorkhas after a long and desperate war, about the beginning of the last century. In rank the Nawars are the first among the Nepalese settlers in Sikkim; they are mostly traders. Next come the Murmis, or chief agricultural class. The lowest class are the Dhamis, or tailors, and next above them come the Kamis, or blacksmiths, and the Sarkies, or tanners. The Nepalese who come to Darjeeling, generally settle down permanently in the district, although some return to their own country after they have laid by a little money. On re-crossing the frontier on the way to their homes, they are invariably mulcted in sums graduated on a sliding scale, nominally to pay for the restoration of their so called caste, which they are supposed to have lost by residing in British Territory; probably the Nepalese Chancellor of the Exchequer could make a pretty good guess as to what becomes of this poll tax.

The probable reasons why so many Nepalese immigrate into British, as well as into Independent, Sikkim are as follows:—In the first place, like the population of the West of Ireland, they are a wonderfully prolific people, and the population of the country has increased to such an extent and so rapidly, that the land can no longer find food for them all. In the second place, they are sure of finding congenial work, good wages, and kind treatment on the tea gardens. Last, but not least, British Sikkim is a regular cave of Adullam for the Nepalese. The Nepalese laws are more than Draconian in their severity; but except for murder, dacoity, and one or two other heinous crimes, no extradition treaty exists between Nepal and British India, consequently once a Nepalese criminal gets safely across the frontier he is beyond the reach of justice. Again, the ordinary Nepalese is never happy unless he is over head and ears in debt, so he generally gives his creditors the slip when they become too pressing. All these causes unite to promote a steady flow of immigration. The Nepalese will live in the same village with the Lepchas, but in a separate quarter of it by themselves.

The *Limboos* are not unlike the Lepchas in appearance, but their skins are more yellow, their eyes are smaller and more oblique. They never plait their hair, but wear it in unkempt, elfin locks. They are exceedingly dirty and gross-feeders, being specially fond of a gorge of pork. Their disposition is just the opposite to that of the Lepchas, and a large proportion of the murders in this district have been committed by them. They make good soldiers, and are said to be equally brave and cruel in battle, neither asking or giving quarter. Their dress consists of loose cotton trowsers and a tight jacket, a sash is worn round the middle of the body and a small cotton cap on the head. They have no caste distinctions, and in religion are an odd mixture of Bhuddism and Brahminism. They cultivate grain, and rear fowls, pigs, and poultry. They once ruled in east Nepal, and they consider themselves the original inhabitants of the Tambour Valley, whither, they say, they emigrated from Thibet. The Limboo language is unlike the Lepcha, and they have no written character. The Lepcha "*Baizouth*" officiates at their funerals and marriages. They burn or bury their dead according to circumstances, raising a mound over the grave and erecting a headstone. If possible they bury their dead on the top of hill.

The *Magars* occupy the lowest levels of Nepal, chiefly to the east of the Kali. The Magar alphabet is of Indian origin, and their religion is hybrid. They are forbidden to eat beef, but are fond of any other meat, and have a great penchant for strong drinks, in which they indulge freely. Their priests are called Dhamis. The Magars are divided into twelve *thums*. All individuals belonging to the same *thum* are supposed to be descended from the same male ancestor, descent from the same mother being by no means necessary.

The *Gunmugs* are a pastoral tribe occupying the higher slopes of the hills in Nepal. They breed large numbers of sheep, and also use them as beasts of burden. They have a language of their own, which differs from that of their neighbours, the Magars, and from that of the Hindu population. They eat beef, and there is a considerable admixture of Paganism in their religion.

The BHOOTEAS, of whom there are so many in the neighbourhood of Darjeeling, and who inhabit a village of their own just below the Chourasta, are divided into several classes:—*i. e.*; the Thibetian Bhootea, or Bhootea Proper; the Bhootea of Bhootan; the Sikkim Bhootea, and the Sharpa Bhootea, a cross between the Thibet Bhootea and the Lepcha. In Darjeeling all these classes, except the very well-to-do, are hewers of wood and drawers of water, taking service as dandy bearers, water carriers, porters, &c. They are a noisy, troublesome, drunken lot as a rule. In the country parts of the district they keep large herds of cattle in the Forest Reserves, and supply the station of Darjeeling with milk and butter. They also cultivate the soil. Both men and women are well and comfortably clad in woollen cloth of their own manufacture, and the women seem to spend most of their time, when not otherwise engaged, in spinning, at which they are great adepts, and they hardly ever have the spindle out of their hands. They profess a sort of depraved Bhuddism, and are very devout in the externals of their religion, but of their morals, the less said the better. They are all followers of the red capped sect of Lamas, but they offer all sorts of propitiatory gifts to evil spirits, and surround their houses with tall bamboo flagstaffs, from which fly cotton streamers covered over with block type prayers for preservation from the "evil one." The well-to-do women love to load themselves with silver ornaments, in which large turquoises are set; these stones are, as a rule, of bad colour and much flawed. They are also very fond of coral beads, which they wear in profusion. Nearly all the women wear a silver or gold amulet round their necks in which is contained either an ornament or some paper with the mystic "*Hom Mani Padmi Hom*" inscribed on it.

Women and men alike are tall and of large frame, though much inclined to run to flesh. Some of the men and many of the women are inclined to be tolerably good looking. Their capacity for carrying heavy loads is marvellous; two maunds weight is a mere joke to them, and there is a tolerably well authenticated story of a Bhootea woman, having carried a grand piano from Punkabari to Darjeeling in three days, and arriving quite fresh at the end of the journey. The men are very fond of putting the shot.

The MECHIS are confined entirely to the Terai, so that the visitor to Darjeeling will have little or no chance of seeing a specimen, unless he regularly stalks one of the aborigines. They are divided into two clans: the Bodas and the Dhimals. Like the Lepchas, the advance of regular cultivation is driving the Mechis out of the district, as, like the Lepchas, they follow the *jhuming* mode of cultivation. They are a stunted and ill-developed race, though living as they do in the midst of dense forest and cane brake, they never suffer from intermittent fever while they continue in the jungle, but once they leave it the malarial poison, with which they have been saturated for generations, finds an exit in fever, and the result is usually fatal. They are a distinctly nomadic, people and each family attends exclusively to its own patch of cultivation, on which they raise cotton, oil-seeds, &c., and they keep a few goats, pigs, cows, fowls, poultry and pigeons, but neither sheep or buffaloes. Their religion consists entirely in worship of the sun, moon, and stars, and of the four terrestrial elements. They have a few household gods to whom they offer milk, honey, parched rice and other products of the earth, and they sometimes sacrifice pigs, goats, and fowl.

As THIBETIANS may often be seen in Darjeeling during the cold weather, a short description of them may be of interest. In a mixed crowd in the bazaar of a Sunday, if you pick out the very dirtiest man or woman you can find, be sure he or she is a Thibetian trader; these people cross the snowy range annually about November, bringing with them rock-salt, yaks, tails, sometimes gold dust, musk, and other commodities of various kinds, besides sheep and goats in large flocks. These they sell, and return laden with tobacco, broad-cloth, piece goods and other commodities, in February and March. During their stay in Darjeeling, they live in small light tents which they bring with them. Their favorite encamping ground is the Lebong spur. It will be observed that there is only one woman in each tent, with five or six men. This is accounted for by polyandry being extensively—indeed almost exclusively—practised by the Thibetians. The young women would be rather fresh complexioned, but for a habit they have of daubing their faces over with a preparation of some sort of gum, which looks like brown lacquer.

CHAPTER IX.

NATURAL HISTORY.

THERE is not an abundance of any kind of game in the hilly district; bears are found both on the higher spurs, and the lower ranges, especially when the maize crop is about ripe. The hill bear is inordinately fond of maize, and at this season many are brought to bay; leopards are common in the hills; and a few elephants and tigers are met with in the Terai. In the Jalpaiguri Division, tigers, rhinoceros, buffaloes, leopards, bears, red stag, sambur deer, and wild hogs abound; a few wolves are also seen.

The game found in the Terai District is hare, jungle-fowl, florican, partridge of two kinds, peacock, snipe, woodcock, wild duck, wild goose, and green pigeon. In the neighbourhood of Darjeeling green pigeons are very plentiful in the rains, and in winter occasionally wood-cock have been shot. In the wooded valleys the barking deer is tolerably plentiful, and an occasional pig may be met with. They have also been shot within a few miles of the station. The inevitable pariah dog and jackal, make night and morn hideous here, as in the plains. There are also an immense number of lizards, scorpions, centipedes, and a small brown insect somewhat resembling the latter, but quite harmless, with this peculiarity that on a touch they roll themselves into a ball so hard and round, one might almost play marbles with them. Snakes are rather plentiful in the forests, few are venomous, although at least four varieties of vipers have been found. Fleas and flies of varied size and intensely rapacious nature, enforce notice by their too pressing attentions, in which they are not at all discriminating, attacking alike "the gentle and the simple," and in every possible way defying all measures taken to circumvent them. There is also the Peepsa, a minute insect that abounds in the valleys on the river banks, and looks no larger than a black speck floating before the eyes. Its nature is eminently blood-thirsty, and its size most disproportionate to its bite.

The leeches may here be mentioned. During the rains they lie in wait for the passenger, whether man or beast. They are generally found in grass jungle and often on the leaves of trees. They are a regular curse to the unfortunate cattle which are turned out to graze in the forests, and it is no uncommon thing to see a whole herd of cattle bleeding profusely from their noses, the result of leech bites. The legs are the favorite place of attack in the human subject, and no boot, gaiter, or any other device has yet been discovered which will keep them out. Fortunately with people in good health the bites give rise to little or no irritation, if only they are not scratched, although in people whose health is below par troublesome sores are sometimes originated by the bites of these pests. There is another and larger variety of leech which appears to have its habitat in the hill streams ; this attaches itself to the noses of drags and ponies high up, and is often very difficult to get rid of. An injection of strong brine will often dislodge the leech.

CHAPTER X.

RIVERS—MOUNTAINS—MINERALS.

THE principal rivers are the *Teestá* and *Mahánada*, which with their numerous affluents, form the main drainage of the country.

The *Teestá* takes its rise in Chalámu Lake in Thibet; it is also said to have another source below Kánchinjangá in Independent Sikkim. After passing through and draining Independent Sikkim, it touches the British District of Darjeeling on its northern frontier, marking the boundary between Darjeeling and Sikkim for some distance, till it receives the waters of the *Great Ranjit*, when it turns to the south, and after flowing through the hill portion of the district, passes through Jalpaiguri and Rangpur Districts, and finally falls into the *Brahmáputra* below Bagwa in Rangpur. It has a course of upwards of 90 miles. The principal tributaries of the *Teestá* within Darjeeling, on its left bank, are the *Rangchu*, which falls into it on the northern boundary,and the *Roli*, which flows through the north-eastern part of the district; and on its right bank, the *Great Ranjit*, which, after flowing through Independent Sikkim, join the *Teestá* on the northern boundary of the district. The banks of the *Teestá* are precipitous; its bed is rocky in the hills and sandy in the plains. The summits of its banks are clothed with forests of *Sâl* and other trees. It it not fordable within Darjeeling District at any time of the year. It is a magnificent stream; a ride along the banks of the *Teestá* through the Darjeeling hills, from Sivak at the base of the mountains, upwards to the confluence of the river with the *Great Ranjit* on the boundary of the district, well repays a lover of the picturesque.

The *Máhánada* has its source near Mahaldirám hill. After leaving the hills, it forms the boundary line between the *Tarai*, and Jalpaiguri to Phansideva, in the extreme south-east of the district. After leaving Darjeeling the *Mahánada* passes through Purnea and Maldah and finally falls into the Ganges at Godagari, just within the borders of the Rajshahai District. Its banks are sloping and in the lower part of the *Tarai*, cultivated: in the hills they are covered with trees and jungle. The bed of the river is rocky or sandy, according as it flows through the hills or plains. There is a strange peculiarity about this river; soon after it emerges from the hills it loses itself in the sandy soil, and only appears again after a distance of four miles or thereabouts, but this phenomenon is only seen during the cold season. The river is fordable only during the cold weather.

The *Great Ranjit* enters the Darjeeling District from the west, and forms a part of the northern boundary, flowing from west to east until it joins the *Teestá*. This river is not navigable, being purely a mountain stream. Its affluents are the *Rangno*, the *Little Ranjit*, and the *Ramman*, these meet it above its junction with the *Teestá.* Its banks are shelving and covered with forest or jungle. Its bed is stony or sandy, as it flows through hill and plain, like the *Mahánada.*

The *Ramman* takes its rise in the Singalila range, which forms the western boundary of the district, separating it from Nepal. It first touches Darjeeling in the extreme north-west of the district, whence it flows along the northern boundary from west to east, until it falls into the *Great Ranjit.* Its bed is also stony or rocky, and it is not fordable at any time of the year.

The *Chota* or *Little Ranjit* takes its rise under the Singalila mountains on the borders of Nepal, and eventually falls into *Great Ranjit* on its right bank. Its bed is the same as all the other rivers, but it is fordable in the dry and cold months in many places. These last named rivers have several tributaries, but they are little more than mountain streams.

The next large river is the *Balásun,* which takes its rise at Jagat Lepcha, a few miles to the south-west of the station of Darjeeling. When it enters the Tarai it divides into two streams, one, called the *New Balásun,* which branches off and joins the *Mahánada* on its right bank just below Siliguri; the original, the *Old Balásun,* continues its course southward until it passes out of the Tarai into the Purneah District. The new channel is said to have been formed some thirty years ago by the Mechis damming up the stream for the purposes of fishing.

Dr. Hooker's description of the mountain scenery of Sikkim,—with the exception that the hills have been competely denuded of forest, to an elevation of about 7,000 feet in most places, in order to make room for tea and other cultivation—still holds good.

The following description is taken from Dr. Hooker's *Himalayan Journal*, page 386, vol. II.

"The main features of Sikkim are Kánchinjangá, the loftiest measured mountain in the world.* It lies in its north-west corner, and rises 28,178 feet above the level of the sea. An immense spur, sixty miles long, stretches south from Kánchinjangá to the plains of India. It is called the Singalila range, and separates Sikkim from east Nepal; the waters from its west bank flow into the Tambar, and those from the east into the Great Ranjit, a feeder of the Teestá. Between these two latter rivers is a second spur from Kánchinjangá terminating in Tendong.

"The eastern boundary of Sikkim, separating it from Bhootan, is formed by the greater part of the Chola range which stretches south from the immense mountain of Dankia 23,176 feet high, 50 miles E. N. E. of Kánchinjangá. Where the frontier approaches the plains of India, the boundary line follows the course of the Teestá and Rangpu, one of its feeders, flowing from the Chola range. This range is much loftier than Singalila.

"The Dankia mountain, though five thousand feet lower than Kánchinjangá, is the culminating point of a much more extensive and elevated mountain mass. It throws off an immense spur from its north-west face, which runs first west and then south-west to Kánchinjangá, forming the watershed of all the remote sources of the Teestá. This

* Except Mount Everest in the Nepal Hills which has an altitude of 29,002 feet. Dr. Hooker wrote the above before this was ascertained.

spur has a mean elevation of from 18,000 to 19,000 feet and several of its peaks rise much higher.

" Sikkim consists of a mass of mountainous spurs. There are no flat valleys or plains in the whole country, no lakes or precipices of any consequence below that elevation.

" Viewed from a distance on the plains of India, Sikkim presents the appearance—common to all mountainous countries—of consecutive parallel ridges, which run east and west. These * * * are backed by a beautiful range of snowy peaks, with occasional breaks in the foremost ranges through which the rivers debouch. Any view of the Himalayas, especially at a distance sufficient for the remote snowy peaks to be seen overtopping the outer ridges, is, however, rare, from the constant deposition of the vapours over the forest-clad ranges during the greater part of the year, and the haziness of the dry atmosphere of the plains in the winter months.

" At the end of the rains, when the south-east monsoon has ceased to blow with constancy, views are obtained sometimes from a distance of nearly two hundred miles. From the plains, the highest peaks subtend so small an angle, that they appear like white specks very low on the horizon, tipping the black lower and outer ranges, which always rise out of a belt of haze, and probably from the density of the lower strata of the atmosphere never seem to rest on the visible horizon."

As we have before remarked, scenery more sublime, more stupendous, more charming, more varied, both of mountains, hills, valleys, and rivers, could not well be imagined. Even a partial survey of these beauties of nature would well repay the traveller for all his toil and trouble.

MOUNTAINS.

This is the appropriate place for giving a list of the snowy peaks as seen from the Observatory Hill, or the North side of the Darjeeling Mall. Looking from west to east are observed :—

1, Kangla.
2, Janu, in Nepal, 25,300 feet, 46 miles distant.
3, Kabur or Kabru, 24,015 feet, 40 miles distant.
4, Kánchinjangá, northern peak, 28,156 feet, 45 miles distant.
5, Pandim, 22,017 feet, 36 miles distant.
6, Narsing, 18,145 feet, 32 miles distant.
7, D 2, 22,520 feet, 46 miles distant.
8, Chomiamo, 23,300 feet, 70 miles distant.
9, 3 or Yakcham, 19,200 feet, 49 miles distant.
10, Kamhenjhan, 22,509 feet, 69 miles distant.

A mass of unnamed snowy peaks are between this and

11, Donkia Rhi, 23,136 feet, 72 miles distant.
12, Sinkam.
13, Narim, 17,572 feet.
14, Dopendikang or Chominnioo, 17,325 feet, 43 miles distant;

to the east of which is the Chola pass.

15, Gipmochi, 14,518 feet, 42 miles distant; and next come the snowy peaks of Bhootan. Between the mountains there is a continuous stretch of snow. The range can only be described as sublimely grand. It is impossible to do it justice in a painting. The only way to form a conception of its glorious beauty is to see it for oneself.

Minerals.

Iron and copper are found, and a little is manufactured by the natives, but in a primitive and perfunctory manner. Coal exists in many places throughout the district; it was first pointed out by Dr. Hooker, who called the attention of the Bengal Government to it so far back as 1849. Since then the seams have been explored by members of the Geological Survey, but no practical use has hitherto been made of the knowledge gained. Lime is obtained by burning calcareous turfa, and quarries of this stone are worked. The turfa rock is nearly all pure carbonate of lime. It is found near the new cart road in Darjeeling, and in several water-courses a few miles from the plains, also on the east bank of the Mahánada, as well as in many other places in and around the district.

CHAPTER XI.

SCHOOLS.

THE climate of Darjeeling is so admirably adapted for children, that the establishment of schools for the education of the sons and daughters of Europeans and East Indians was contemplated as far back as 1842. The advantages of having these schools in such a splendid climate, and within now so easy a distance of Calcutta, can scarcely be over-rated.

St. PAUL'S ENDOWED SCHOOL was started in Calcutta in 1845, and removed to Darjeeling in 1864. Its affairs are managed by a Committee of gentlemen, all, or most, of whom are resident in Calcutta. Its situation is superb; one of the best sites in the neighbourhood, its grounds are extensive and laid out in great taste, it has the most English park-like appearance of any estate in the station, and commands views of the whole of Darjeeling. The sanitary arrangements are under the immediate supervision and control of the Civil Surgeon of Darjeeling; the health of the boys we know from personal knowledge to be excellent, and the domestic arrangements are on a liberal scale. The school is calculated to accommodate 150: it is quite full, and numbers of applicants have had to be refused admission as scholars.

The Head-master is R. Carter, Esq., B. A., Queen's College, Oxford, who is assisted by a large staff of masters.

The charges are very moderate, being only Rs. 10 per mensem for day-scholars, and Rs. 25 for boarders.

The DIOCESAN GIRLS' SCHOOL was established in 1875, and is already making great progress under the excellent management of Miss Roby. The charges are Rs. 10 to Rs. 16 per mensem for day-scholars, and for boarders Rs. 25 per mensem. We can personally testify to the admirable manner in which both young and old are cared for. The Resident Civil Surgeon of the station, under whose medical control the school is, is noted for his extreme care and judicious supervision. That young children should be sent to school at all in the plains, when such an admirable institution and healthy place is open to them, is a matter of wonderment. The journey now to Darjeeling costs so little, and the place takes so little time to reach, it cannot be doubted, when its merits are more fully known, but that it will become the most popular of Hill Schools.

The CATHOLIC BOARDING and DAY SCHOOL (Loretto House) also receives young ladies on extremely moderate terms. Report speaks highly of its admirable internal management, and of the devoted attention of the Lady Superioress and her assistants. We do not know exactly on what terms it receives pupils, but believe they are slightly higher than those of the Protestant Girls' School.

This school, although recently enlarged, is not large enough to accommodate all the applicants for admission.

The grounds are spacious and retired, and extremely healthy.

In connection with this school for girls is one for little boys, standing a bit apart from the Convent. The boys are excellently cared for and well taught the rudiments of English, writing and arithmetic. St. Joseph's Seminary is a comparatively new school. It is unfortunate in not having any playground to speak of. The boys are well taught, and the school has always been successful at the Entrance Examinations of the Calcutta University.

W. NEWMAN & CO.'S
POPULAR INDIAN HANDBOOKS.

W. NEWMAN & CO.'S
INDIAN GUIDE BOOKS.

The Tourist's Guide to all the principal Stations on the Railways of Northern India, from Calcutta to Peshawur, Karachi, and Bombay; and from Bombay to the North-West by the Rajpootana Railways. Including also notes of Routes to some of the Himalayan Hill Stations. Fifth edition. Crown octavo, 153 pages, in paper cover, Rs 2: in cloth, with coloured map. Rs 3.

Newman's Railway Map of India. The most useful Map of India published for Merchants, Tourists, and Military Officers. Size 24 by 22 inches. Coloured, and mounted, folded in book form, Rs 3. Or, Mounted on Rollers and Varnished. Rs 4.

Handbook to Calcutta, Historical and Descriptive. With a plan of the City. Second edition. Crown octavo, 250 pp., in paper cover, Rs 2-8; in cloth, Rs 3.

Newman's Pocket Map of Calcutta. Size 10½ by 10 inches, coloured, and folded. As. 8.

Guide for Visitors to Kashmir. Being an intinerary of all the principal routes in Kashmir. By JOHN COLLETT. With a large route Map. Rs 4.

Index Geographicus Indicus. A Popular Gazetteer of India. By J. FREDERICK BANESS, F.R.G.S., F.S.,S.C., (London), *Surveyor and Chief Draftsman, Geographical and Drawing Branch*. With eight coloured Maps of the Chief Divisions of India on the scale of 64 miles to 1 inch. In one volume, super-royal octavo, half bound in roan. Rs 12.

Newman's Indian Bradshaw. A Guide to travellers throughout India. Published monthly. As. 8.

CPSIA information can be obtained at www.ICGtesting.com
Printed in the USA
LVOW09s1715140316

479091LV00008B/343/P

9 781293 331